MW00633339

STRIP, TRIP AND SHADOW QUILTS

for People Who Don't Have Time to Quilt

Audrey Brooker

by
Marti Michell

BOOK II of the "QUILTING FOR PEOPLE WHO DON'T HAVE TIME TO QUILT" Series

FEATURING:
No Pattern Pieces Required, "Make Any Size Block You Want" Grid System, Sew-Before-You-Cut Patchwork, All Quilts Made with Strips and Squares, More Machine Quilting Techniques

QUILT DESIGNS INCLUDED:
Amish Shadows/Roman Stripes, Overnight Success Quilt, Joseph's Coat Borders, Railroad Crossings, Sunshine and Shadows, Trip Around the World

©1990 by Martha G. Michell. Published by American School of Needlework, Inc., ASN Publishing, 1455 Linda Vista Drive, San Marcos, CA 92069
ISBN: 0-88195-284-2   Printed in U.S.A.   7 8 9

Before You Begin........................

IF THIS IS BOOK TWO, WHAT HAPPENED IN BOOK ONE? Book One, "Quilting for People Who Don't Have Time to Quilt" (ASN #4111), is the introductory book for these efficient, accurate, wonderful fun techniques. Both my publisher and I would like to believe that you already have Book One and its companion book, "Designing Quilts with Strips and Squares" or that you will rush to get them. In fact, while we are creating a series of books, we are both committed to making each book stand alone without being overly repetitious. Usually the second book in a series implies it is more difficult. In fact, these quilts are not more difficult, just different.

So Where To Begin?

It is important to start with a clean slate, sometimes called an open mind. If you've ever thought of quilt making as cutting out hundreds of little pieces, one little piece at a time, and then sewing them back together, one little piece at a time, forget it! One of the first things you are going to learn is that many traditional quilt designs can be translated into accurate, time-saving strip sewing methods. You will begin to learn how to recognize designs which can be adapted.

It may sound strange, but everything you can **Sew-Before-You-Cut** is more accurate, faster and easier. This is one way of describing strip piecing techniques. Strip techniques are the backbone of this book. You will quickly learn to appreciate these techniques by actually doing them yourself in the quilt making section of this book. It is hard to do them justice in words. In this case, a few minutes of action is worth a thousand words.

All of the techniques in these books were developed so that you can enjoy making quilts for people to use—no strings attached. We will be making quilts that can be finished in hours, not months or years. The techniques include multiple cutting, strip piecing and chain piecing. We encourage you to maximize these methods with machine piecing and machine quilting skills. You will be learning the techniques by making specific quilts, but many of the methods can be adapted to other quilts. You'll notice that the phrase "quick and easy" hasn't been used. In fact, the methods are both quick and easy, but we try not to say those words very often because many people automatically think "quick and easy" means big pieces and shabby workmanship. Not so with these techniques. To discourage your friends from that kind of negative thinking, we recommend you learn to talk about loving the clever methods and the accuracy and meticulousness of the techniques. Later, when people exclaim over your quilts, please say, "Thank you", but **never** say, "Oh, these? They were easy!"

A Little Review

A large introductory section in Book One includes explicit answers to the questions most commonly asked by beginning quilters. For people who want a short answer instead of the explanation, there is a "nutshell synopsis" method for answering many of the questions. That is, a quick answer followed by a detailed version. In this book, instead of repeating the entire "Before You Begin" chapter, we will just review the short answers. If you want a more complete reference, please see Book One.

LEARN TO THINK IN PATCHWORK GRIDS

You can make lovely quilts quickly, but you do have to be selective. You must understand that every quilt that you've ever seen can not be made using these techniques. As you look at the pictures, you'll notice no curved seams or complicated angles. You will begin to understand that all of the quilts you are looking at can be drawn on a grid. The most frequently used shapes in patchwork are squares, right angle triangles and strips. All of them can be drawn on a grid such as graph paper.

The next important thing to look for is repetition in the order of the fabrics. That is when strip techniques can be used to the maximum. Squares, of course, are just strips cut so their length is the same as their width.

There are so many popular quilts that are made with just strips and squares that all of the quilts in both Book One and this book are made with those two basic shapes or, we could say, are made from strips. That doesn't mean that everything in the finished quilt is a strip. It just means that the first cut on every piece is a strip.

THERE ARE NO PATTERN PIECES

You do not need pattern pieces or templates if the quilt design can be drawn on a grid (like graph paper). Instead, you will learn to use the grid to represent measurements and eliminate pattern pieces. Perhaps the most important feature of quilts drawn on grids is that you decide what size pieces to work with. You are not confined to fixed pattern piece sizes and only one finished size block. The size of the first strip you cut determines the scale and finished size of the project. For example, in this illustration (**Fig A**) there is a grid 4 blocks wide by 5 blocks high. If each block represented 1", the shape would be 4" x 5"; if each represented 2", the piece would be 8" x 10", etc.

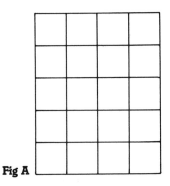

Fig A

Strip techniques in cutting mean that for every block in a repeating grid pattern, you will cut a strip. The strip will be as wide as the finished size of the block plus ½" (two ¼" seam allowances). The strip will be as long as you want or is convenient. I prefer 27" cut on the lengthwise grain but will sometimes use 45" on the crosswise grain. Anything longer than that tends to get unruly.

For people who measure in centimeters, the grid system crosses that barrier. To convert to centimeters, just let each block represent your favorite size strip in centimeters.

WHAT ABOUT FABRICS?

1. Fabric selection is very important. It does much more to set the mood of the quilt than the pattern. Because most people aren't used to combining lots of different fabrics, the tendency for beginners is to overmatch everything and end up with borderline boring quilts. Look for variety in the fabrics you are combining. Not just in the colors, but in the scale of the prints, the type of prints and the density. Pay special attention to the relationship of light, medium and dark colors in your quilt design.

Learn to stand back and look before you buy or cut the fabrics selected for a quilt. We all tend to select fabrics when we are only an arm's length away. But we rarely look at the finished quilt from that distance. Instead, it is viewed from "across the room". The fabrics can look very different then.

2. It is true that 100% cotton is the generally preferred fabric of quilters. You can use any fabric, it is your quilt, but unless there is an overwhelming reason to use other fibers, stick with cotton for now.

3. Contrary to nearly every article or book you have read, prewashing your fabrics before using is not mandatory. I prefer the crispness of non-washed fabrics for machine piecing and quilting. I do test fabrics for both colorfastness and shrinkage before beginning and, of course, if there is bleeding or shrinkage beyond the 2% to 3% allowed by industry standards, I pre-wash that fabric or select another fabric. 2% to 3% translates to ¾" to 1" in a yard or ¼" to ⅓" in 12".

Because nearly everything I make starts with strips, it is easy to test by cutting a 2" x 12" strip of all of the fabrics I have selected for a project. Then holding and squeezing them under hot, running water both saturates them with water and allows me to see if there is any color bleeding. Then I take the strips back to the ironing board and iron them dry. It is the heat on the wet fibers that makes them shrink. Then I measure and compare them to the original size and to each other.

If one fabric shrinks considerably more than the others, it is a greater problem than if they all shrink the same little amount.

4. I prefer to cut strips on the lengthwise, not crosswise grain. Because most dress pattern pieces are marked "Place on the lengthwise or crosswise grain", we tend to think there is no difference. Tug on the same piece of woven fabric in both directions and you'll see that the lengthwise grain is much firmer. It is also much straighter. Strips cut on the lengthwise grain do not fray or stretch as much as those cut on the crosswise grain, **Fig B.** They are easier to keep straight while pressing and they help camouflage visually distorted prints.

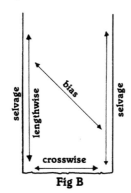

Fig B

Sometimes sheer economics will cause me to cut on the crosswise grain. That is, I only need a little bit of a particular

fabric. When you cut lengthwise strips from a quarter yard of fabric, you can hardly call it a strip. When using a directional fabric design, its demands will always override any grain line cutting rules.

HOW MUCH FABRIC DO I NEED?

The question was, "How much do I need?" I have found that what I need and what I want are two different things. My policy has always been to buy as much as I could afford. Once you start making lots of quilts, you have a real appreciation for sewing from a stockpile of fabric.

Just as there is no single fabric yardage requirement to make a dress, there is not one answer for how much fabric it takes to make a quilt. Here are some rules of thumb. Just the backing for a queen/double quilt requires 6½ yards. So, if you add fabric for seams and some latitude in cutting, I say you need a total of 10 yards for the surface of a not too complicated queen/double quilt. Following the same line of thought, you need a total of 12½ yards for a king and 6½ yards for a twin. Almost everyone agrees having extra is better than agonizing over running out. More and more I find I use my extra yardage for pieced backs for quilts or in pillow cases. I put them on top of the quilt propped against the bed, then I don't have to fight the pillow tuck battle.

Two important things about the amount of fabric are:

1. Learn not to panic or quit if you run out of fabric for a particular plan. Look at it as an opportunity to be creative in quilt making and problem solving.

2. Relax about having "just the right amount". With so many variables, expecting to come out even is not realistic.

All estimated yardage requirements used in this book are based on 45"-wide fabrics. When I'm buying speculatively, the least amount I ever ask a clerk to cut is 27" (¾ yd). That's not an arbitrary amount; the reason is that almost everything I do starts with a strip and because I cut my strips on the lengthwise grain whenever possible, 27" has turned into my standard strip length. (If you buy ¼ yard pieces, the lengthwise grain will only cut a 9" strip!) Also, I like to use many different fabrics in most of my large quilts and I make quite a few small quilts. Using fabric those two ways, ¾ yard of a single fabric is almost always enough. Of course, if you are making quilts with only two or three fabrics or cutting long one piece borders, you need to buy more.

If I'm crazy about a fabric and/or think I might want to use it as a border on a large quilt, I buy 3½ yards. That is the most I would need to cut a king size border with mitered corners on the lengthwise grain. And since I prefer unpieced borders this becomes a real issue for me. As you use these longer cuts, remember to save a long wide piece along one selvage for borders, **Fig C.**

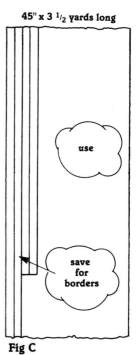

45" x 3 ½ yards long

use

save for borders

Fig C

3

WHAT SIZE IS A QUILT?

How much fabric you need to buy is really a function of what size quilt you are making. When you make quilts for fun, that is, just because you want to, they can be any size. Quilts are used so many ways besides bed coverings that another view is to say that when you run out of fabric, it determines the size of the quilt.

Size is only crucial when you are making a quilt for a specific bed or place on the wall. Then, lots of personal choices could alter the dimension. It's best to measure a specific space or bed and work with your design to get as close as possible. Remember to add 2" to 4" in each direction for the "dry shrinkage" or "take up" that occurs when quilting. Be aware that as you get into planning quilts for specific sizes, compromises often have to be made.

When measuring the bed isn't an option, I use these quilt size guidelines. Except for the crib size, they were developed by adding 9" for a pillow tuck at one narrow end and a 13" drop to the other three sides of standard mattress sizes.

Crib—small 30" x 45"; large 40" x 60"
Twin—65" x 97"
Double—80" x 97"
Queen—86" x 102"; queen/double 84" x 100"
King—104" x 102"

ACCURATE CUTTING IS CRUCIAL

Some of my quilt-making friends love the quilting most, some the piecing process, but I don't know anyone who loves the cutting. Yet accurate cutting is the first crucial step in accurate patchwork. I love a good pair of scissors and I wouldn't be without them for my routine sewing, but one of the reasons the strip methods are so effective comes from the introduction of rotary cutting systems in the mid 1970s. The Rotary Cutter looks like an advanced pizza cutter. It must be used in conjunction with a special protective mat and is most effective with a rigid, thick acrylic ruler for long straight cuts!

With the rotary cutting method, you can be faster than with scissors, but more importantly, you can be more accurate than with scissors. You can accomplish the cutting processes outlined in this book with a ruler, pencil and scissors, but you'll save time measuring, save time cutting and be more accurate with the rotary cutting method.

To be effective cutting strips with a rotary cutter, you need a strong straight edge. There are many different acrylic rulers 5" or 6" wide and 24" long. They are usually printed with a grid on the ruler surface that is very helpful in assuring accuracy. Most rulers also have angles and other special printed features. With just a little practice, you'll be comfortable cutting nearly any straight line geometric shape with just a ruler and rotary cutter, further eliminating the need for patterns, templates, and tedious tracing. Throughout this book, measurements are given in sizes for cutting.

Tips for Using the Rotary Cutter

The blades are very sharp. All of the brands currently available have guards. Make sure they are in place when the cutter is not in use. This protects both you and the blade. If you drop the cutter or accidentally cut across a pin, the blade often becomes nicked. Then instead of cutting the fabric where the blade is nicked, it perforates the fabric. The blades are replaceable, but the need can be minimized if you will just keep the guard in place. A fresh blade will cut 6 to 12 layers of

fabric easily with very little pressure. Bearing down too hard is not necessary and can do irreparable damage to the protective mat. It's harder to accurately fold and stack 12 layers of fabric than to cut them. When cutting, the blade side, not the guard side, goes immediately next to the acrylic ruler. Cut away from you, not toward your body, **Fig D**.

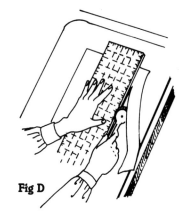
Fig D

To get straight strips, it is imperative that the ruler be perpendicular to the fold on folded fabrics and/or parallel to the selvage. The first cut is usually trimming off the selvage (cutting strips on the lengthwise grain) or straightening a store cut edge (cutting strips on the crosswise grain). To make a strip, the next cut is the second side of the first strip. It requires changing hands, going to the other side of the mat, or turning the mat. My favorite method is to cut the first strip left handed—not really hard with the good ruler—and the rest right handed which is my favored hand. Then I don't have to change table sides. Take advantage of the grids on the mat and on the ruler to maximize your accuracy.

OTHER TOOLS

Most other tools are probably already in your sewing supplies. Good small scissors, a seam ripper, thimbles, hand-sewing needles, etc. You will probably want to add some specialized quilting tools like removable fabric marking pens and pencils, smaller acrylic rulers and squares soon. Put a steam iron and ironing board next to your sewing machine.

The Sewing Techniques In Theory

How you actually sew the pieces together unlocks the secrets of "Quilting for People Who Don't Have Time to Quilt" techniques. Eliminate the idea of making a quilt piece by little piece. Remember, **everything you can SEW-BEFORE-YOU-CUT is more accurate, faster and easier!**

It's almost revolutionary. It's different from anything you've been taught. This book stresses it repeatedly. You will see how to look at quilt designs you want to make and analyze what pieces you can Sew-Before-You-Cut.

ANALYZE

The old patchwork ways of cutting and sewing one piece at a time, incorporated very little thought. You do need to think ahead and organize a little for these methods to be most effective. Actually the first thing is to analyze the pattern and develop a plan. This will be covered repeatedly in the project section of this book.

We will even emphasize analysis and thinking ahead in cutting. For example, often the first two strips that are going to be sewn together are also the same dimension. If you place the fabrics right sides together when you cut, you have eliminated a step and, as a bonus, the strips are more accurately positioned for the seam.

STRIP PIECING

The first step in Sew-Before-You-Cut is usually strip piecing. When you study a quilt design and see the same two squares of fabric side by side repeatedly, you realize that you can either cut lots of each square and sew them together or you can cut a few strips of fabric as wide as the squares, sew the strips together and then cut the sewn strips into pieces as long as the square, **Fig E**. Likewise, you will quickly learn to recognize three, four or more fabrics repeating in a way that sewing strips of those fabrics together is advantageous. That is what this is all about.

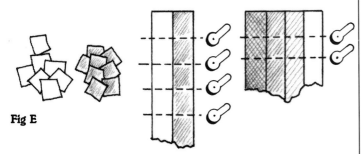

Fig E

With a little practice you will see how to put these simple concepts to work to make you look like a miracle quilter. Your friends will not believe how fast you can do patchwork. You are not required to share these secrets. If, however, you decide to be generous and tell about your newly learned skills, NEVER, NEVER say it's easy. Say it's clever, say it's smart, say it's a brilliant new technique you've learned, but never say it's easy. It is, of course, we just don't say so.

The Actual Sewing

SEAM ALLOWANCE DATA

The recommended seam allowance is ¼", using 10 to 12 stitches per inch. It is not necessary to backstitch the seams as you will stitch across most ends almost immediately. If you are new to patchwork, you may not have entered the world of the ¼" seam allowance yet. After using ⅝" seam allowances in dressmaking, the first ¼" seam will look impossibly thin. Remember, many ⅝" seam allowances survive being trimmed smaller than ¼", turned inside out, and poked. Not only is the ¼" seam allowance adequate for patchwork but if it is necessary to make a narrower seam allowance, don't worry until you get below ⅛". Most people who do miniature patchwork, (finished pieces smaller than ½"), regularly use a ⅛" seam.

On many sewing machines the outside edge of the presser foot is exactly ¼" from the center of the needle hole. An easy way to measure is to put a tape measure under your presser foot, **Fig F**. Put any inch mark at the needle. Put the presser foot down. If it's ¼" wide, you're lucky. If it isn't, you'll have to find some other way to calculate the ¼" seam. For now, when you are just doing strips, a guide on the throat plate or a piece of tape can be lined up to show where to run the edge of the fabric.

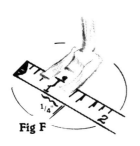

Fig F

There's More to Perfect Patchwork than a ¼" Seam Allowance

In the final analysis, it's the size of what you see that is really important, not the size of the seam allowance. The seam allowance is there to keep the sewing threads from ripping out and to allow you to make adjustments if necessary. The object is to have a perfect 1" square, for example, in the finished patchwork, not to have a perfect ¼" seam allowance. You can over emphasize sewing exactly ¼" from the cut edge. It's fine when it works and if you have both a perfect finished piece and perfect seam allowance, you can feel very smug. But the most important thing is perfect size finished patchwork.

SOMETIMES IT'S CONSISTENCY THAT COUNTS

It is also true that in all the quilts in this book or in any quilt where you are using only strips, even as they become squares, it is consistency that counts. If following the edge of your presser foot results in a seam just a little larger or smaller than ¼" all that happens is that the finished item is just a little larger or smaller, as long as all of the seams are the same.

All measurements given in this book are cut measurements. We always talk about the cut size and cut accurately; then by sewing consistently, the finished sizes are consistent shapes. This is not true with complicated, multi-shaped pieces and curvy lines. With those shapes, you must know exactly what size seam allowance is on the pattern and double check while sewing to be sure you are really stitching on the correct line. This is why people who love being productive, love quilts using "Sew-Before-You-Cut" techniques.

MATH VS. PATCHWORK

Math is an exact science—sewing is not. Patchwork is a cross between them. Paper patterns and measurements that are mathematically correct may not end up exact when interpreted in fabrics. Learning how to spot clues for when things might not be working and learning how to make necessary adjustments comes with practice, but examples are discussed in the project section.

PRESSING—THIS IS NOT AN OPTION!

As you embark on patchwork, it is smart to make your iron one of your best friends. My preference is a steam iron. When pressing patchwork seams, both seam allowances go in the same direction, not open as in dressmaking. Usually, press them toward the darker fabric. Time spent carefully pressing is time well spent.

When I am pressing a set of strips, I usually put the strips across the ironing board instead of end to end, **Fig G**. With

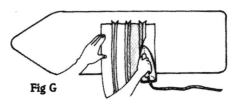

Fig G

the seam allowances right side up, I hold onto the fabric with my left hand and put the iron down on the other edge of the strips. With the weight of the iron holding the right hand side of the fabric, I put just a little tension on the left side. That causes the seam allowances to stand up and, with the steam iron, I can press them down flat. Keep the strips straight, don't press curves into your strips. It is easiest when all seams go in the same direction, but many times the instructions are press towards the darker fabric. That often means that seams need to go in opposite directions on the same strip. Sometimes you can press from each side in towards the center. Sometimes you have to hold the strip at the end and work your way down the middle. You do what you have to do to get it right!

With the philosophy that once is not enough, I then turn the strips over and press from the printed or right side of the fabric. The object is to eliminate any tiny folds I might have pressed into the seam. Tiny 1/32" folds don't seem like much until you multiply that times 2 for each seam and times 4 or 5 seams for a block and times 10 or 12 for the number of blocks. I admit to being a fanatic about perfect pressing.

During the project section, you will see how directional pressing becomes a crucial part of ease and accuracy in sewing. You will learn how to plan pressing to your advantage. This may not seem very flashy, but it simplifies your stitching life and gives you lots more time for the fun stuff. Along this line, a side effect of directional pressing is what I call "automatic pinning". It is best described in Make the Four Patches, page 35.

Typically, you will press between each step. You may want to put a low pressing area right beside the machine, but I don't mind getting up to press. I usually have sewn so many strips or sets together while at the machine that it gives me a chance to stretch.

Short Cut Pressing

Sometimes finger pressing can postpone pressing for one step, but be very careful about trying to go longer than that without pressing. Using the combination of your fingers and the presser foot tension to hold the seam allowance in place, you can stitch across the most recent seam adequately. You have to decide which is more important to you, perfect, flat seams or saving minutes on every quilt you make the rest of your life. Everything is a trade off.

THE "SECOND CUT"

This is really your first opportunity to put the Sew-Before-You-Cut theories to work. Now that your first strips are cut, pieced, and pressed, you make the cut that forms the second dimension of the patchwork piece. The width of the strips

formed the first dimension. Again go to the rotary cutter and mat and perhaps switch to a shorter acrylic ruler. Accurately cut a new common line across the sewn pieces. This assures more accurate dimensions on the pieced unit.

In essence, this means you are working with larger pieces and it is easier to be accurate with larger pieces. Stated another way, 1/16" error is a much greater percentage error on a 2" cut piece than an 8" piece.

CHAIN PIECING

Strip piecing is the process of sewing two strips together. Chain piecing means continuously feeding under the presser foot and sewing the same pieces in the same order without cutting the thread. We often chain piece strips, but chain piecing more commonly refers to piecing after the "second cut". Watch carefully for any obvious visual differences. There are many visual clues. Seams and cut edges should line up perfectly, for example.

SOME TIPS ON RIPPING

My stitch length is relatively small, and I truly don't like to rip, so I try to avoid the need. You can avoid ripping by never making a mistake or by not caring when you do. Each of us has to set our own level of perfection.

If you must rip, the gentlest way is best. On one side of the seam, cut every 6th stitch or so. A little experimentation will let you know if you can get by with cutting every 7 or 8 stitches. Then turn the fabric over and pull the thread on the other side. When you cut at the right frequency, the thread just pops out as you pull. Go back to the first side and brush away the clipped threads. I can do about 10" per minute or 1/100th of a mile per hour!

In another ripping technique, pull one thread, gathering the fabric on the seam, until it breaks. Then go to the other side of the fabric and pull the opposite thread until it breaks. Proceed back and forth until the seam is removed. This is faster and neater, but it is harder on the fabric and more likely to cause distortion.

Sometimes straightening a seam is necessary because there is an equal error in both pieces of fabric. As long as the new seam allowance is wider than the old one, straightening simply requires a new seam, no ripping. The old stitching can stay in the seam allowance.

Getting on Good Terms

Patchwork is easier when you are in control of these geometric terms.

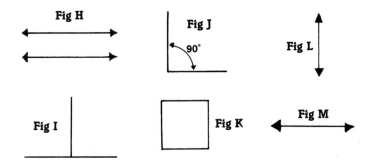

Parallel—lines extending in the same direction at the same distance apart so as to never meet, **Fig H**.

Perpendicular—a straight line at right angles to another straight line, **Fig I**.

Right Angle—an angle of 90 degrees—also called a square corner, **Fig J**.

Square—a four-sided figure having all of its sides equal length and all of its corners right angles, **Fig K**.

Vertical—straight up and down, **Fig L**.

Horizontal—parallel to the horizon, perpendicular to vertical, straight across, **Fig M**.

Lengthwise—in the same direction as the length.

Self Teaching Projects

PLEASE READ THE **WORDS** IN THIS BOOK.
I have a friend who says, "I only read the pictures!" and I cringe. While we are proud of our pictures and illustrations, some of the best information is communicated with words.

PLEASE READ **ALL** THE WORDS
I know this sounds pretty demanding, but we've worked hard to be concise and avoid repetition. So, even if you think you don't want to make an Amish Shadow Quilt, that is the only place where the best way to add borders is discussed. That is information you need for almost all quilts.

PLEASE **MAKE** A QUILT
No matter how many pictures, illustrations or words you read, there is nothing like making the quilts to understand what you've read!

About the Quilts in this Book

In Book One the quilts were presented progressively so that the techniques that you learned in the first quilt became the foundation information and every quilt added more knowledge to that base. There was a lot of emphasis on unit blocks. Unit blocks are the "smallest common denominator," the combined pieces that are put together over and over, assembly line style, to make the process go quickly and efficiently. And all of those unit blocks were made with a set of strips sewn together to represent every row and then cut at right angles to make a new, larger, ready-to-sew piece.

In this book all of the quilts are still based on cutting strips to begin, but they incorporate methods unique to the particular design. It is necessary to develop each quilt in more detail and the knowledge base is not frequently transferred directly to other designs. In other words the unit blocks are not as easily recognized and the strip techniques are somewhat different for each quilt. You will see, however, that you begin to find the repeat units more quickly with each quilt.

8

Amish Shadows..................................

The first quilt in this book, which we will go through in step-by-step detail is the Amish Shadow. The text quilt is approximately 54" x 68" finished, a nice size for a wall quilt or throw. You may choose to make a dramatic full-size quilt with the same procedure and number of pieces. The pieces would be larger, but they are proportionate to a bed. Instead of inserting the full-size measurements through the copy for the text quilt, the changes necessary for the full-size quilt are on page 18.

My suggestion would be to read this text all the way through, then come back and start making the full-size quilt. When you come to any size reference, turn to the full-size quilt section and make the proper substitution.

The Amish Shadow Quilt is a traditional quilt with a very contemporary look. Most people call it Amish Shadows when all the fabrics are solid colors, and Roman Stripes when it is made with printed designs. When you look at this quilt, it's easy to think it must have more shapes than only strips. While the narrow strips are the interesting part, anyone can see they are held together with some large triangles. Maybe, maybe not. My favorite technique for making those triangles is a slightly different **Sew-Before-You-Cut** method that starts with strips!

Amish Shadows is the perfect quilt for people who think they don't like quilts. The contemporary look of the solid colors and the bold dramatic design possibilities make it perfect for the person who doesn't like the image of quilts with tiny prints and flowers. College students are crazy about this quilt. It is a wonderful quilt for waterbeds. It is masculine enough to suit most men.

It's perfect for the quilt maker who is afraid of picking colors, because it's almost impossible to make a mistake. It's grand in full-size on beds, but it's absolutely wonderful in a smaller size wall hanging. The versatility of arrangement means an Amish Shadow quilt can be a tailor made wall hanging for any shape wall. One of the really nice things about the Amish Shadow quilt is that it tends to just happen rather than involve a lot of planning. Generally the colors that you pick set a mood, and help determine how you are going to arrange the blocks.

You will discover that the Amish Shadow quilt has unlimited design possibilities, but until then, let's work with exact instructions for a quilt with 48 squares, to be referred to as the "text quilt."

Fabric Selection

First things first. A lot of people think that they don't want black in their quilt. Have faith. Make the first quilt black. It's so quick. And if you don't like it when you're through, somebody will think it's a great gift. Black is wonderful for the background of this quilt. Black is very forgiving. It makes the colors sparkle and look good. It seems that other colors used in the background demand much more particular fabric selection. If you are saying, "I won't make this quilt if I have to use black," there are options. Looking at the pictures in the book, you'll see very attractive quilts with navy, gray or muslin backgrounds.

Next, select assorted solid color fabrics. Seven is the **absolute minimum** and ten is more likely to please you with the final results. The colors may vary widely. The multi-colored combination is the safest quilt because it is not restricted, it can be used anywhere. If you feel more comfortable in one color group than any others, color coordinate a bit, but be prepared that when you coordinate, you begin to confine where the quilt can be used. When you over coordinate, you risk making a quilt that is downright boring. When you make a full-size bed quilt, there is no limit to the number of colors you can comfortably use. It doesn't matter if you have only one strip of a color in a quilt. An occasional strip of polished cotton makes a lovely accent.

If you simply can't be sold on solid colors, make the Amish Shadows with prints and you'll have Roman Stripes. (See the photograph of two "Overnight Success" quilts on page 23 for ideas.)

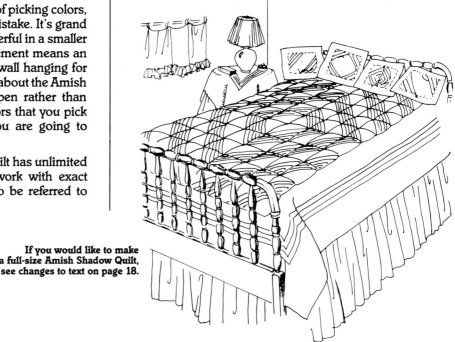

If you would like to make a full-size Amish Shadow Quilt, see changes to text on page 18.

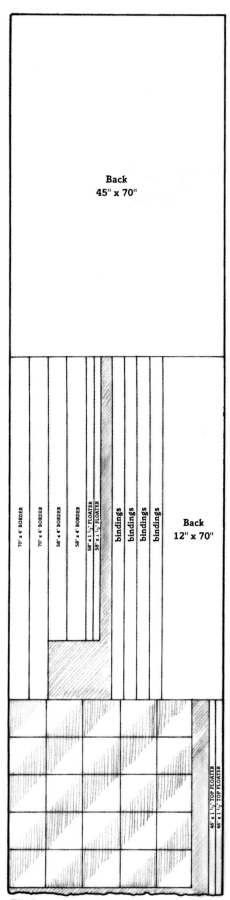

Back
45" x 70"

70" x 4" BORDER
70" x 4" BORDER
58" x 4" BORDER
58" x 4" BORDER
58" x 1½" FLOATER
58" x 1½" FLOATER
bindings
bindings
bindings
bindings

Back
12" x 70"

46" x 1½" TOP FLOATER
46" x 1½" TOP FLOATER

Fig A

Fabric Requirements

For the "text quilt" with 48 squares you will need 5½ yds of black background, border and backing fabric (**Fig A**) and 35 to 40 assorted color strips 1½" wide by 45" long. It is advantageous to use the same fabric for the quilt's backing and for the background fabric on the quilt front. Otherwise, you need 4 yds of backing fabric and 3½ yards of background fabric, both with lots of scrap. For the colors cut a few strips from 7 to 10 collected solid color fabrics or purchase ¼ yd each.

Cutting, Sewing, and Pressing the Strips

DISSECTING THE PIECED TRIANGLE

At first glance, it looks like we should have pattern pieces that look something like this (**Fig B**). They are strips, but look at all those funny angles to cut and try to match. Remember, Sew-Before-You-Cut? It is one of our most important phrases. Couldn't we sew sets of strips together and then cut triangles (**Fig C**) and get the same look?

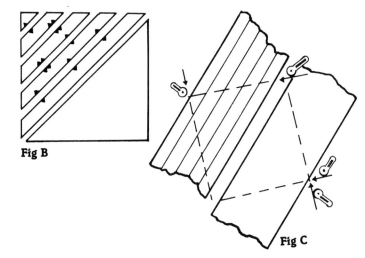

Fig B

Fig C

CUTTING THE STRIPS

For a wall quilt, 1½" wide cut strips are very nice; that's 1" wide finished. If you use larger strips, the matching triangle is so large that it demands more quilting. With the 1½" cut strips, the resulting triangle can be left unquilted.

EVEN WHEN IT'S NOT A RULE, THERE ARE ALWAYS EXCEPTIONS

You have read that cutting strips on the lengthwise grain is one of my all time high recommendations. However, because you need such a small amount of each color, this is a perfect example of where it is more logical to cut strips on the crosswise grain. Remember, measurements for pieces are given in cut sizes.

Thirty-five crosswise strips are just enough, that is seven sets of five strips 1½" x 45", but cutting five more strips for another set is a good idea. It allows a little more flexibility in laying out the quilt, gives you a chance to throw out a set you don't like, and the extras can always be made into a matching pillow or other small item.

SEWING THE STRIPS

You will be sewing the strips together in sets of five. When selecting the five fabrics for each set, don't worry about making each one "pretty." In other words, "clash" a few colors. Put a surprise in one or some of the sets. One set of strips can even be very dull! The biggest mistake in the multi-color quilt, is to divide the colors into little color families. If all the rust-beige-brown strips are sewn together and all the green-blues are sewn together, it looks like strips from two different quilts. Random is one of my favorite guideline words for how to get an attractive arrangement. Because it is unstructured, many people are uncomfortable with "random." It means without order or plan. You might even try shaking the strips in a bag, reaching into the bag (no peaking), removing one at a time and sewing them together in the order in which they are removed. There can be some real surprises, but it is random. Sometimes the surprises are pleasant. You may randomly put together great combinations you wouldn't have ever thought of on your own. The diversity in the sets of colors eventually helps tie the quilt together.

Later you will see that alternating the triangle as you cut sets of pieced strips appears to double the number of combinations. This is pointed out dramatically in the color photo at the top of page 22. The two small pieces in this picture are fun, quick decorator pieces that are easily made in an evening with just two sets of basic strips. The one on the left is called "Great Balls of Fire," a tribute to rock and roll. The one on the right is called "Journey to the Center of the Earth." The interesting thing is that they were made from the same sets of strips.

Notice that the outside color of the strips will become the largest, most dominant. In this particular case, there were very strong, bright, dominant colors on one side of the set and very quiet colors on the other side. The alternating triangles were cut and two sets that looked nothing alike resulted. You have to look carefully to see that all the teeny red tips on the "Journey" piece were cut from the same strips as the great huge red strips in the "Balls of Fire" piece.

Get comfortable at the sewing machine and start sewing those strips together. Just make long straight ¼"-wide seams. Make it easy, steady sewing. Don't stretch and pull strips, just guide. See Seam Allowance Data on page 5. If you can learn to start each strip down 1" from the previous strip, the little wasteful triangles at the end of the strips are offset and will disappear, **Fig D**. More importantly, you get an extra pieced triangle from every set of strips.

PRESSING THE SETS

When the sets are all sewn together, press the seams all in one direction. This is a crucial step. You could have cut perfectly, sewn perfectly and then if you are not careful, you will press this set of sewn strips into a rainbow-like curve. (See page 5 for Pressing—This Is Not An Option.) So press carefully, moving your iron along in a straight line. Do not allow your arm to move in an arc. If you have included polished cottons, they can be stubborn about pressing to one side. It may be necessary to give in to that fabric and let it lie the way it wants.

CHECKING THE NEW WIDER STRIP SIZE

When all of the strips are sewn and pressed, go back and check the finished width. Five perfectly cut 1½" strips sewn together with perfect seam allowances and pressed perfectly flat will yield a strip 5½" wide. Measure your strips in several places. If they measure 5½", pattern piece A (on page 19) is perfect for you. After measuring, many people will discover they have their own, one and only, unique strip width. (Measurements between 5¼" and 5¾" are most likely. One of the beauties of this quilt is that it doesn't really matter!)

Oh yes, to make a quilt that is identical in size to the mathematically correct quilt, you need 5½" strips. But there is no magic in the mathematically correct quilt, so a little larger or smaller doesn't matter. You just need to know what is happening and know how to make necessary adjustments.

How did it happen? You might have created a unique width during any of the previous steps. The point is that when each strip is slightly wider or slightly narrower than expected, the finished set width can vary from 4¾" to 6¼", **Fig E**. Because the block size and ultimately the quilt size is determined by the size of the largest right angle triangle you can cut from your set of strips, that range of finished widths would result in very different quilt sizes.

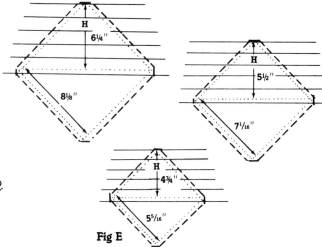

Fig E

Did you notice the phrase "pattern piece" a few paragraphs back? That's right, there is a pattern piece. You can also learn how to cut right angle triangles with the rotary cutter and acrylic ruler, or use the pattern and acrylic triangle in combination. If you are using the pattern piece and your finished set of strips is a one and only unique width, the dimension of your triangle pattern will have to be changed.

Fig D

The "H" line of your triangle should be carefully adjusted to match the most common width in your sewn strips. (The corner of the triangle has been blunted in the pattern to make the exposed strips as accurate as possible when the squares are complete.)

If you have just an occasional narrow spot, and the rest of your strips are wider, adjust the pattern to the majority width. If there are narrow areas in the strips where you must compromise because your strips aren't as wide as your pattern in a spot or two, sacrifice the point. Because your base strip is most visible, always make sure it is full width! Then check to see that the amount you are sacrificing at the point is still within the seam allowance. If it is not, check the pressing. You may have a little fold that when pressed flat will make the strips wide enough. You can take out a seam in the strips and make the set wider or throw out that particular triangle and be grateful you made extra.

A right angle acrylic drafting triangle can be a very helpful template tool. Just tape the correct size pattern to the back of the triangle to establish the exact base line for positioning the triangle, **Fig F**. The blunt corner on the paper pattern, not the point of the acrylic triangle, will line up on that edge of the strip. Then you can cut with the rotary cutter. But, **"to cut now or not to cut now?"** —that is the question. Read both options for "Making the Squares" before you decide.

Making the Squares

OPTION ONE
The obvious and more traditional method proceeds with cutting right angle triangles separately and seaming them into squares.

Cutting Triangles from Pieced Strips
Using your one and only unique triangle pattern and following the cutting diagram (**Fig D** on page 11), you should be able to cut seven triangles per set of strips. (You will probably get eight if you staggered your strips when seaming.) Handle the cut triangles gently during and after cutting. Once the strips are cut into triangles, all of the newly cut edges are on the true bias and are very stretchy. Cut 48 pieced triangles.

Cutting Non-pieced Triangles
Using the same triangle pattern, the solid triangles will be cut with the legs on the **straight** of the grain as shown in **Fig G**. You'll need 48 non-pieced triangles. If you have the rotary cutter and protective mat, use it now for cutting the triangles. The shapes are much more accurate if the fabric does not have to be lifted while cutting.

Piecing the Squares
If everything has been cut perfectly, the pieced triangle will lie face down on top of the non-pieced triangle, all edges matching, and you simply stitch a ¼" seam along the long edge. Chain piece for more efficiency as in **Fig H**. Leave the pieced triangle on top while stitching. Usually the non-pieced triangles are the more accurate. If a slightly different size is the only problem, just center the smaller triangle over the larger. You will minimize the error by absorbing some of it into the seam allowance at both ends of the seam.

For minor distortion, use the original triangle template and double check the outside dimension before stitching. If after making a few squares, you discover major distortion, it may be necessary to go back and check the accuracy of the triangles before stitching. Slight errors in cutting can make big distortions in the finished squares.

Another way to inspect the sewn squares is to make a NEW template of the finished size square without seam allowances and use it to mark the seam lines for the next step. On the wrong side of the pieced square, line two corners of the template up with the diagonal seam and "square" the other corners, **Fig I**. In the next step, when the squares are sewn together on these lines, the distortion will be corrected. This is only necessary if you are extremely finicky or if things have gone very poorly.

Now You Have Squares—or this Quilt's Unit Blocks
When you open the triangles to make a square, it should be a perfect square. Press the seam allowance toward the non-pieced half. (If you later decide to make an Amish Shadow quilt with a light background, you may want to press toward the pieced triangle.) After pressing, take time to cut off the dog ears and threads. It will eliminate bumps and make the back of your quilt much neater.

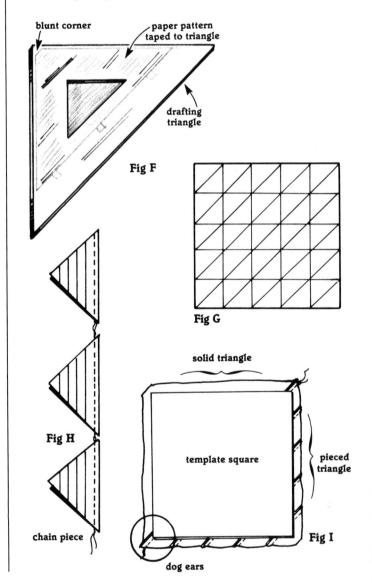

blunt corner

paper pattern taped to triangle

drafting triangle

Fig F

Fig G

solid triangle

Fig H

template square

pieced triangle

chain piece

dog ears

Fig I

OPTION TWO — MY FAVORITE

The most accurate and fastest technique incorporates making bias strips and sewing them to the pieced strips **before** cutting triangles. Remember, almost always, anything that you can **Sew-Before-You-Cut** saves time, is more accurate and is easier. Using this technique, you will be stitching the seam that makes the square before cutting the triangles. Don't let the word bias make you edgy. It is a four letter word that you need in your sewing vocabulary and sewing skills.

The bias strips are cut 5½" wide **or** your one and only, unique, strip width, **Fig J**. Use a right angle triangle to establish true bias. I put the leg of a large acrylic right angle drafting tool (or many acrylic rulers have a 45 degree angle line) along the selvage and then cut the bias edge with my rotary cutter, **Fig K**. Then use a wide strip template along the bias edge to measure the proper width and cut background fabric bias strips that wide and as long as possible. To facilitate cutting, you may want to fold fabric at a right angle to the newly cut bias edge and cut through two layers.

Select a bias strip as long or longer than the pieced strip. Place the right sides of the bias strip and the pieced strip together and machine stitch ¼" from both long edges. Now use the same triangle pattern to mark alternate triangles as shown, **Fig L**. Position the long edge of the pattern on the long seamed edges of the fabric. The seam allowance was included in the pattern so put the edge of the pattern on the cut edge of the fabric just as you would if it were not already sewn. Make sure the seam line of the pattern is on the actual stitched line at both ends before cutting. This is the most important positioning for accurate squares. (If you prefer, cut away the seam allowance on the long edge of the pattern and place the seam line—the new pattern edge—on the actual stitched line.)

If using scissors, cut carefully on marked lines. With a rigid template, a rotary cutter and protective mat, you can position the template and cut, eliminating the marking step. Because of slight distortions when sewing, it may not be possible to have the diagrammed common edges of these triangles actually be common. That is, when the long edge of the pattern is properly positioned, it may be necessary to make slightly separate cuts for triangles that theoretically have a common side.

Just as in Option One, if you didn't stagger the strips while piecing or your width is extremely wide, you'll only get seven triangles, four with the base strip on one side and three on the other. Because the outside strip is the dominant color, make sure you start with the hypotenuse placed along the one you like the most.

To conserve fabric, some of your first bias strips will not be 45" long, but they still work! Using your one and only unique triangle pattern, mark as many triangles on the short strips as possible, **Fig M**. When sewing the seams, stop stitching just past the marked triangles. After stitching and cutting the first short strip, remove any scrap bias and repeat with another short background strip to finish the pieced strip, **Fig N**.

After cutting, unfold and press toward the dark fabric. The stitching threads that run across the tip of the triangle will just pop out. You should have perfect squares.

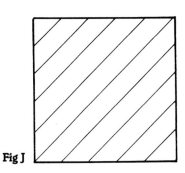

Fig J

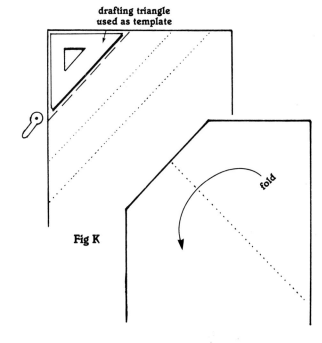

drafting triangle used as template

fold

Fig K

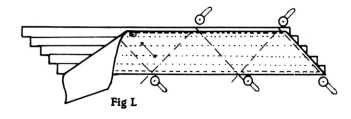

Fig L

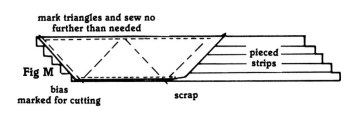

mark triangles and sew no further than needed

pieced strips

Fig M

bias marked for cutting

scrap

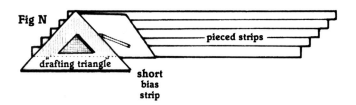

Fig N

drafting triangle

pieced strips

short bias strip

Here are examples of
different ways that
Amish Shadow blocks
can be arranged.

This Is the Fun Part!!!

No matter which method you used, it would be a good idea to make sure your squares are square. A large square acrylic measuring tool is the easiest way. Take advantage of the tool's square corners and markings to check for squareness and consistency. If everything isn't perfect, don't despair, you can still make some adjustments.

ARRANGING THE SQUARES

You will probably want to make a trial arrangement of the pieced squares on the floor. And guess what, after you arrange it, you will undoubtedly rearrange it again and again. If you have made an arrangement that you like a lot and you have an instant camera of any sort, it's a nice "insurance policy" to take a picture. It is also a way to compare arrangements and an aid for arranging it exactly the way you like the most. Don't be surprised when casual observers want to make suggestions.

The most traditional setting is very rigid and has all the pieced triangles in the same corner of each square. See the Navy Blue Amish quilt on the lower right of page 14 and in color on page 21, made with only 25 squares. Even if you use this setting, you will want to arrange the entire quilt in order to get good placement of colors. I have seen some photographs with all the stripes in the bottom corner, and some the top. Even if there is a way it is "supposed" to be, it seems as though when it's your quilt you can hang it the way you choose.

It's likely that you will see beyond the traditional arrangement. The dynamic diagonal structure of the block cries out for you to try some more contemporary abstract arrangements. The Amish Shadow block has a very strong diagonal line developed by the seam of the two triangles. Look at the illustrations and pictures for other possible arrangements. If you want to flex your abstract design ideas, this is a good starting point. If you have extra strips, you may want to make some smaller projects like the wallhangings in the upper left photo on page 22, the wallhanging in the lower left photo on page 21, or see the illustrations with the Overnight Success quilt in **Fig C** on page 25.

When placing the squares, an important thing to remember is that one of the things that makes these quilts "work" is the rhythm of the movement of the colors. You could look at a hundred black and white drawings of arrangements of these diagonally dominant squares. The important thing, however, is how YOUR squares work and how they play against each other and what you "see" when you look at them.

As you work, stand back and look. Is there an objectionable concentration of color in one area? Is it well balanced? Are there any mistakes in the order of the blocks? Don't let yourself get crazy with rearranging, the best look is a relaxed, random look. When you are satisfied with the arrangement, it's time to start sewing the blocks together. Sometimes it is the title of a quilt, together with the arrangement of fabrics, that makes it work. Great Balls of Fire, in color on page 22, is a perfect example. I would never put all those red strips together if I didn't want to make a statement.

If you prefer to be more traditional, but not completely traditional, the text quilt is 48 squares because it makes a beautiful rectangular Barn Raising setting. Most quilt blocks have a name. Sometimes the way a group of quilt blocks is put together has a name. Barn Raising is the name typically

Fig O

given to a quilt that is arranged with concentric diagonals, **Fig O**. The Log Cabin block is the most famous block used in the Barn Raising setting.

Bull's Eye Versus Open Centers
Some people feel that triangles set so that all four striped halves touch, look like a bull's eye. They say, "Never, never, never do it." Other people find empty corners objectionable. On a rectangular Barn Raising like the text quilt, you will either have a bull's eye center or empty corners. Remember, it's your quilt, you decide.

If you want the Barn Raising setting in a square, it only took 36 blocks to make the gray quilt with desert color strips shown in color on page 24. A square Barn Raising can have an open center and filled corners in the same set, see **Fig P**.

While most of the design diagrams show only squares that incorporate one pieced triangle and one plain triangle, feel free to make a completed square of background fabric or of stripes if it is appropriate for your design. If you are planning to machine quilt, you may want to piece a solid background square with two matching triangles so there is a seam to "ditch" your quilting in.

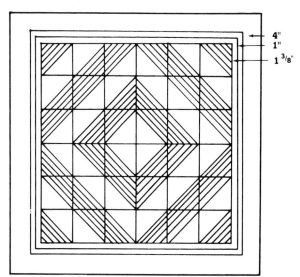

Fig P

4"
1"
1 3/8"

singles | row 1 | row 2 | pairs | pairs of pairs

Fig Q

pairs of pairs of pairs | etc.

Fig R

Stitching Squares Together

When you have settled on the final design, it is easiest to move straight from the surface where your layout is to the sewing machine. Stitch the pieces together in small segments. My favorite method is to stitch pairs, then pairs of pairs, etc. as illustrated in **Fig Q**. It is always tempting to do long rows and try to put the long rows together—but resist. It is easier to make any necessary adjustments when working in smaller segments. Working this way minimizes the number of seams that must match when making the next seam. Seam allowances exist for two reasons. One is to hold the stitched seam in place and the other is to absorb discrepancies or make alterations as you proceed to put additional pieces together.

See **Figs Q** and **R** for one construction plan and note that at this point, three seams is the most you've had to match in any one seam. To finish, add one set of eight squares to the end of a set of sixteen squares. Then the last seam across the middle is the longest single seam in the quilt. As you start assembling the squares and pressing the seams, handle the quilt gently and keep the sections as wrinkle free as possible while you work. As you piece any quilt top, you have many vulnerable places—bias edges, raw edges etc. Treat them as gently as possible.

CHAIN PIECING

Take advantage of chain sewing techniques whenever possible. For example if the quilt is laying on the floor, decide to piece the first and second rows together. Lay each square in row 2 right side down on its matching square in row 1 which is right side up. Now stack all pairs in order from top to bottom of the quilt. Starting with the pair of squares from the top, feed the square sets consecutively through the sewing machine in the order stacked. If the squares aren't quite the same size, center the smaller on the larger so that some of the error goes into all four seam allowances. Do not cut the thread between the newly pieced squares, but leave them chained, it keeps them in the proper sequence. Repeat with the additional rows. You may even want to mark the top and number of each row before starting to stitch, while you have all the squares laid out. I safety pin a little piece of paper on mine, **Fig S**.

Top
row 1

Fig S

PRESSING AND AUTOMATIC PINNING

When the squares are "chained" together, it is easy to press seams in alternate directions and have the squares properly positioned for the next series of seams. Stitch each pair of squares to the pair of squares in the row below, resulting in stitched pairs of pairs.

Match seams carefully as squares are sewn together. This means match the seams of the squares, **not** the seams where the strips were pieced. Lots of people think those are supposed to match. Not only is that a good way to drive yourself crazy, but if you accomplished it, the quilt would tend to look a little sterile. A good word for the lack of strips being aligned at the seams is refracted!

Remember, the objective is for the finished size or the exposed part of the squares to be the same size. If you have to make adjustments in the seam allowance to accomplish this, you do. Sometimes people think the most important thing is to take an accurate ¼" seam allowance. No, no, no! It's nice if it should work out that way, BUT if your squares are NOT the exact same finished size, and you take perfect seams, there is no way that quilt will be flat.

Finish assembling the quilt. DON'T pick up your quilt top to show it off UNTIL you have sewn on a border that will stabilize the edges. This is a good rule with any quilt top, but this particular quilt is loaded with stretchy bias edges and it is especially important not to handle it excessively until the first border is attached.

Borders

SELECTING THE BORDERS

In the "text" quilt, the borders are: 1½" cut (one inch finished) black border, the same size contrasting second border (color of your choice), and a 4" to 5½" cut third border, with a separate matching binding. (The last border on the gray quilt was cut 6" wide to allow for finishing the quilt by turning the front to the back and hemming. I prefer separate bindings, but the front to back technique is explained in No Separate Binding, page 44.)

Hopefully you will be inspired to experiment on your own. Selecting the borders is another design statement. If you want to experiment with borders, now is the time. When the quilt is all pieced, put it back on the floor and try strips of different fabrics and widths. You'll see how different colors in the border make your quilt express different moods.

Hard and fast rules rarely exist in quilting, but cutting a contrasting border for this quilt that is wider than the original strips is rarely effective. You can put multiple contrasting strips together to get the illusion of a wider strip. Once you've decided on the border arrangement, you're ready to cut the borders. Our directions are for what we call blunt corners, **Fig T**. The effect of mitered corners goes practically unnoticed on this quilt, and doesn't justify the extra time nor fabric. In other words, if you want them, you undoubtedly know how to figure border lengths etc. and we won't muddy the waters with a second set of instructions.

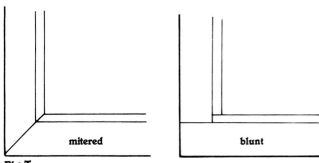

Fig T

ADDING THE BORDERS

It is a common practice to cut a long strip of fabric for the border and just sew it on until you run out of quilt. If your quilt is perfectly square at every corner and the dimensions all match, that may work.

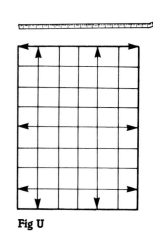

However, when you are adding the first border pieces, you have a golden opportunity to correct imperfections in the quilt. Measure the length from point to point, **Fig U**. If the opposite sides match, you're good! If they don't match, don't despair, now's your chance to correct them. Look at the quilt. If you have lots of bias edges on one side of the quilt and that is the long side, you should make the borders match the shorter edge. You do not want to stretch it as you add a border. When you let go it would pull up and make the border ruffle. Always ease the longer side to match the short. The most important thing is that the opposite borders are the exact same length.

Fig U

Cut the first pair of lengthwise borders the EXACT desired finished length plus seam allowances (preferably on the lengthwise grain of the fabric with no piecing, see **Fig A** on page 10). There is an important trick in adding the borders. The trick is to make the quilt FIT the matching borders. The easiest way is to mark quarters on the border and quarters on the quilt and match them. Ease in any extra fullness on a long edge. If necessary divide quarters into eighths. If wrinkles appear to be developing, consider altering some of the quilt seams to correct the length. Whatever you have to do, make the quilt fit the border. This means you are controlling the stretchy bias edges, not vice versa. Press seams toward borders.

Now measure the crosswise ends including the attached borders. Decide what the best width is. Calculate what it should be. Compromise if necessary, but make the opposite sides the EXACT same length. This is the length you should cut the crosswise set of borders. Once again, make the quilt fit the borders. When you do, the quilt with its first set of borders should have matching side to side dimensions, not just at the corners, but all through the quilt.

Continue adding the borders, always putting the lengthwise borders first and the crosswise borders second as you work on each set. Press your border seam allowances. Now find a wall and pin or tape your quilt top on it so that you can stand back and enjoy!

Quilting instructions start on page 40.

Amish Shadows
full-size queen/double

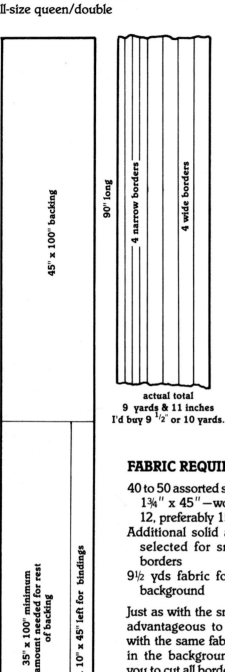

45" x 100" backing

90" long

4 narrow borders

4 wide borders

**actual total
9 yards & 11 inches
I'd buy 9 ¹/₂" or 10 yards.**

35" x 100" minimum
amount needed for rest
of backing

approx. 10" x 45" left for bindings

45" minimum for squares

Fig V

FABRIC REQUIREMENTS

40 to 50 assorted solid color strips, 1¾" x 45"—work with at least 12, preferably 15 colors.

Additional solid accent color as selected for small border or borders

9½ yds fabric for backing and background

Just as with the smaller quilt, it is advantageous to back the quilt with the same fabric as that used in the background. That allows you to cut all borders, binding and backing pieces on the lengthwise grain without piecing, **Fig V**.

Cutting and Sewing the Strips

The strips are cut 1¾" wide. If you are staggering the strips when sewing, drop each strip 1¼" lower as you start to stitch. Staggered ends should result in six triangles per strip instead of five when the ends are straight.

The mathematically correct width for five strips sewn together is 6¾". Don't forget that it is easy for that measurement to vary as much as ¾" in either direction. Use Pattern B (page 19), adjusting the pattern to fit your own one and only measurement, if necessary. For Option Two in making the squares, the bias strips would also be cut 6¾" wide or adjusted to your average width of pieced strip sets.

The finished squares will be 8¾". Both triangles could use some additional quilting. One of the easiest, but still effective ways to quilt this would be diagonal rows in both directions. The quilting would actually form an "X" in every square.

BORDER MEASUREMENTS

In **Fig W** you can see one quarter of two different renditions of the queen/double Amish Shadow. On the right, the interior part of the quilt would be made with 48 blocks, approximately 8¾" square. That means the interior section of the quilt would be approximately 52½" x 70" which fits the top of the bed nicely, but would require very wide borders. The one shown is a very pleasant arrangement. The first border is 2½" matching the background. Then a set of three contrasting, 1¼" borders, followed by the nice wide 7" frame.

two full size quilt options –
one quarter each shown

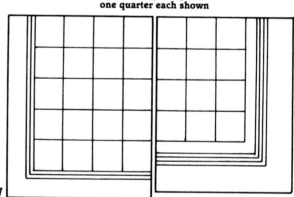

Fig W

On the left, instead of 48 interior blocks, we are showing 80. That is 8 rows across and 10 down. Should you choose this option, it would require 70 to 80 of the 1¾" strips to begin the quilt. The finished interior would be about 70" x 87½" and the same simple border used on the text quilt would be a very nice finish.

Roman Stripes

Roman Stripes is the same as Amish Shadows except made with prints. Probably the muslin and print version in color on page 21 could be called Roman Stripes. Look at the Overnight Success quilts for examples of a similar design with all print fabrics.

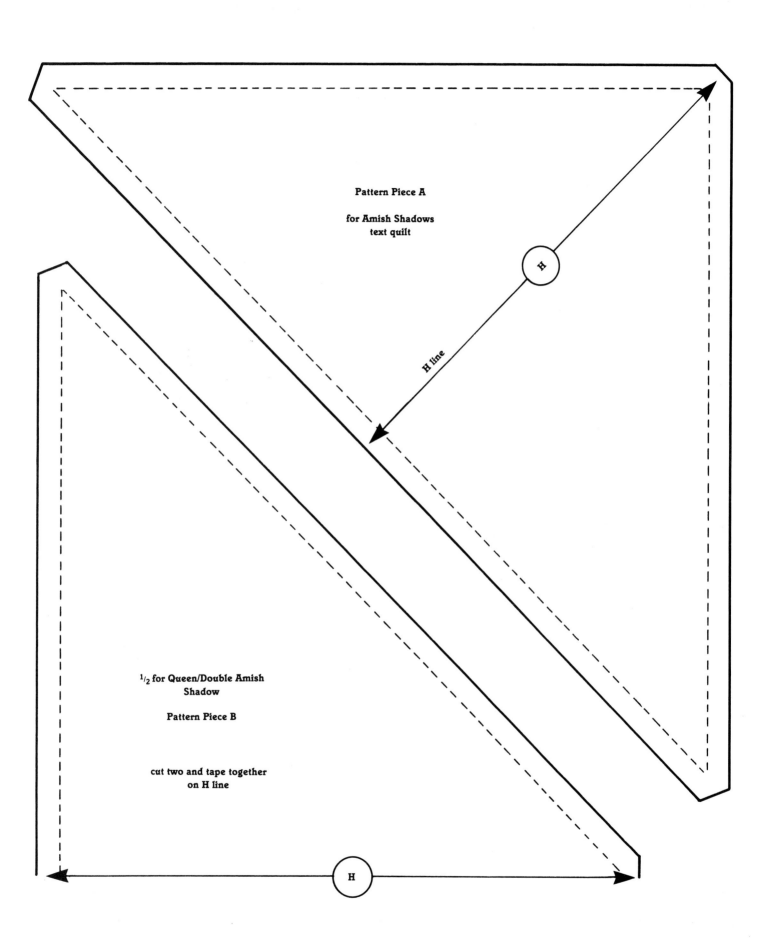

Pattern Piece A

for Amish Shadows
text quilt

H line

H

1/2 for Queen/Double Amish
Shadow

Pattern Piece B

cut two and tape together
on H line

H

Overnight Success Quilt.............................
A Crib Quilt, Wall Hanging or Table Cloth
approximately 42″ square

This quilt is similar to Roman Stripes. In the Overnight Success variation, the fabrics are also all prints, but the strips are all random width instead of uniform. To increase the mix of fabrics, a slightly different technique is used for constructing the squares. This is an ideal quilt to practice "stretching" your color themes and learning to mix prints with more flair and daring. If the colors are too similar, the quilt languishes.

FABRIC REQUIREMENTS

½ yd of dominant color for unpieced triangles, plus more for binding, backing, etc. if desired. Try not to select a fabric with a directional pattern.

¼ yd of fabric for first border, to be cut on crosswise grain. Pick one fabric with lots of colors for the border and then you can select any fabric that has any of those colors to go into the pile for strips.

Batting and backing 1¼ yd each.

Select 10-12 or more fabrics for strips. It is really the combination of the border and background prints that give the quilt its color direction. One way to select strips is to select fabrics that look good with either the border or background. At the same time, exclude any fabric that looks really ugly with either. But don't pick all fabrics that are pretty

and blend perfectly. That kind of quilt usually goes beyond borderline boring. Select a good variety of colors—even a few "clashers"—to keep the eye moving and interested in the quilt. Don't forget when you cut those fabrics into narrow strips and stand back a few feet, they don't have nearly the same impact as when you are looking at the fabric on the bolt. Cut at least 36 assorted strips between 1″ and 2″ wide, very few 1″. This is another place where cutting on the crosswise grain is sensible.

MAKING THE UNIT BLOCK
Make Pieced Fabric

Piece strips of fabric together in random order. Make sure you vary the colors. This is sometimes referred to as string piecing. Then press the string pieced fabrics carefully. Keep strips straight. I repeat, keep strips straight while pressing. In effect, what you are doing is sewing striped fabric. The stripes must be parallel. Think about buying printed stripes. If the stripes were not parallel, and were supposed to be, it would cause many problems in sewing. The finished size of the string pieced fabric needs to be a total of at least 35″ long and 45″ wide, which should be enough for both the borders and triangles. Even though we have illustrated this as one full piece, the strips can be sewn together in smaller sections and will actually be easier to handle.

(continued on page 25)

Above:
Sunshine and Shadows Monochromatic Square Crib Quilt – Project Four
Antique Sunshine and Shadows – Project Four

Left – right:
Amish Shadows Wallhangings
in creative arrangements – Project One

21

Left: **Amish Shadows Wallhangings: Great Balls of Fire** and **Journey to the Center of the Earth** – Project One

Below left: **Amish Shadows Text Quilt** – Project One

Below right: **Amish Shadows Wallhanging** by Stacy Michell – Project One

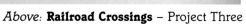

Above: **Railroad Crossings** – Project Three

Above right: **Railroad Crossings,** before and after changing the setting triangles – Project Three

Below: **Overnight Success Quilts** – Project Two
Twin Size and Crib Quilt, Wallhanging or Tablecloth
Both with Joseph's Coat borders

Above left:
Amish Shadows –
Project One

Above right:
**Peach and Sea Foam
Crib Quilt** –
Project Five

Left:
**Glendale Gardens
Trip Around the
World** –
Project Five

24

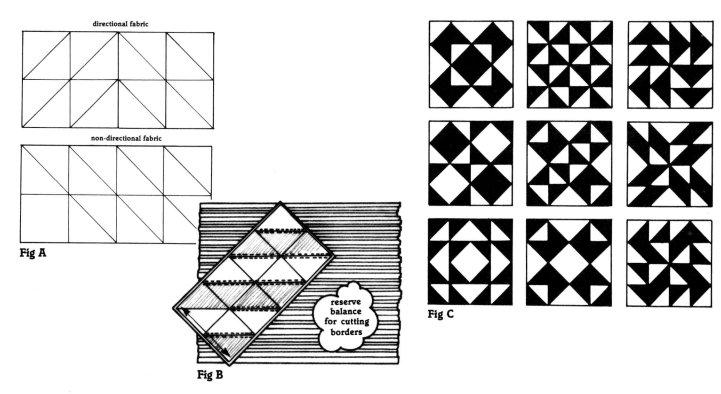

directional fabric

non-directional fabric

Fig A

reserve balance for cutting borders

Fig B

Fig C

Mark Sew-Before-You-Cut Squares

Mark eight 8½" squares on a grid format on the wrong side of the fabric you have chosen for the non-pieced triangles. Add diagonal lines through center of each square. If you have selected a fabric with a one way design, mark half of the diagonals in one direction and half in the other, **Fig A**.

Sew-Before-You-Cut the Triangles

Lay fabric with drawn squares right side down on top of the string pieced fabric. In **Fig B**, the marked fabric is hanging off the edge of the pieced fabric. This is done to conserve larger continuous pieces of fabric for the border. After you sew the first several seams, cut the sewn sections and reposition the remaining square of marked fabric. The diagonal lines go the same direction as the strips and should parallel them. Don't forget they are now horizontal lines. Pin and stitch ¼" on both sides of all diagonal lines as in **Fig B**. If your presser foot is not an accurate ¼", you may want to mark the seam allowance and stitch on the line. These seam lines do need to be straight or the square will not lay flat.

Strictly as an aside, if you look again at **Fig B**, you can see that this is a variation of Option Two in Amish Shadows, page 13. In that method, bias strips were cut the exact width of the pieced set of strips and sewn together on both sides. In **Fig B**, by looking at the grain line arrow and the stitching lines, you can see that the seams are on both sides of a bias strip, it is just an uncut bias strip. **Sew-Before-You-Cut** works again. In case you are wondering why we didn't use this method with Amish Shadows, the difference is the random width pieced strips. It doesn't matter how wide the strip next to the seam is, so the seam for the triangles can be anywhere.

Cut on all **drawn** lines. Open the seamed triangle and press seams toward unpieced triangle for squares. Examine the pieced strips at the diagonal seam. There may be some very narrow strips of fabric, but that is not a problem. Save the extra pieced fabric to later make the pieced border.

Arrange Squares and Piece Desired Design

You may use any arrangement. Sixteen-Patch designs where

each square has 2 triangles are fun. For this particular item, a more symmetrical selection is usually most effective. There is already so much random feeling, the strength of the diagonal block gets lost in an abstract arrangement. Any quilt made from perfect pieced triangles can be imitated with these blocks that are half stripes, half background fabric. See possibilities in **Fig C**.

Piece in pairs, then pairs of pairs to make a square, then four squares. It's easier to match and manage.

Borders
MAKING THE JOSEPH'S COAT BORDER

Even though the border will be made using strip piecing techniques, the casual observer looking at your finished quilt will think you have cut each piece individually and studiously selected their position. One of the potential failings of strip piecing is having repeats become very obvious. This is the perfect quilt for practicing random arrangement and here are a few tips for becoming more effective.

It is easier to disguise several short repeats than one long one. When you do cut matching sections, long or short, make sure you reverse direction with some sets, or split the set apart and add several different strips to break the pattern, **Fig D**.

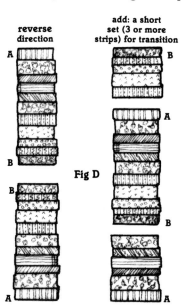

reverse direction

add: a short set (3 or more strips) for transition

Fig D

Press the strips carefully, with all seam allowances going in the same direction. After determining the width of the border (string pieced border shown was cut 4" wide), cut across the strips, making sure the seams stay perpendicular to the edge of the ruler. They should be the length of the side of the quilt you are working on plus 10"-12" to allow for the miter.

ADD BORDERS, INCLUDING JOSEPH'S COAT BORDER

For the first border, add a 2" cut strip all around. The second border is the 4" Joseph's Coat Border. Stitch to each side

stopping ¼" from the end of the quilt so that one border can be pressed flat and one folded back at a 45 degree angle, making a mock miter. Piecing of strips will not match at miters! Stitch in place by hand with an invisible stitch. Trim away excess fabric.

You may quilt and bind as desired, but machine quilting is the only way you can have a true Overnight Success.

Twin Quilt Size

Willing to spend two long or three regular evenings for a twin size quilt? Follow the same instructions except change the grid size for the squares to 9½" and make 32 squares.

Add two narrow borders before the string pieced border. Then add the string pieced border and the final border. Cut measurements for the width of each border are in the twin quilt diagram, **Fig E**. The borders on the quilt shown were added Quilt-As-You-Sew style after the interior section of the quilt had been layered and quilted. (See quilting section, page 42.)

Materials needed for twin-size quilt:
Equivalent of 2 yds of 45"-wide string pieced fabric. It is not necessary to be continuous.
½ yd first border
¾ yd second border
1 yd dominant fabric for unpieced triangles
1 yd third plain border
4½ yds backing fabric
Twin-size batting

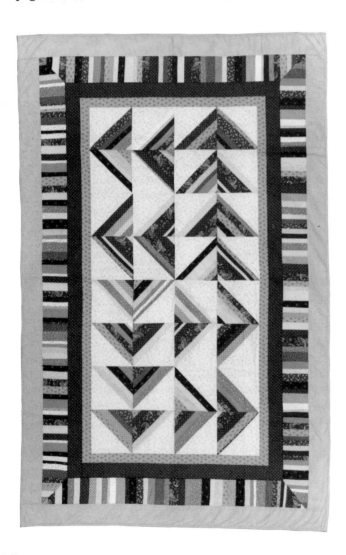

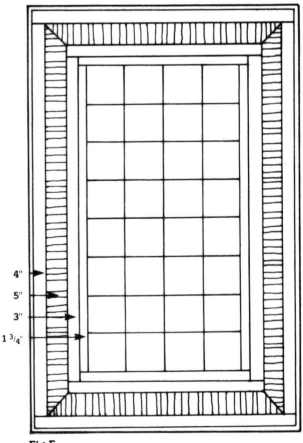

4"
5"
3"
1 3/4"

Fig E

Fig A Straight Set

Fig B Diagonal Set

Railroad Crossings ....

This is an interesting quilt because the design is really in the setting strips and the block position is just plain squares. In addition it is made with a diagonal set, which adds greatly to the visual interest of the quilt, but also has different construction techniques than straight set quilts.

When blocks are set on point instead of resting flat on a side, it is a diagonal set. The rows developed by the blocks and the setting strips go diagonally across the quilt. Either turn your head or turn the book to see the rows more easily. At the ends of the rows there are setting triangles. All of a sudden, you may feel like you need patterns. I have said that everything in this book is made from strips or squares and the setting triangles are no exception. See all the details later in the **Secret of the Setting Triangles**, page 30.

One of the interesting things about this book is that many of the quilts get diagonal movement from the fabric placement design, and have the feeling of diagonal set quilts, but in reality are straight set quilts. With this quilt, we have to make the diagonal set, **Fig B**. See how uninteresting this design would be if it were made with a straight set, **Fig A**.

FABRIC REQUIREMENTS

These are basically scrap quilts, so you would probably make them from collected fabrics. If you are buying new fabric, you might buy the dominant fabrics, the squares and borders, and make the strips from scraps. Buy ½ yd for the outside

border on the larger quilt. Any of the other borders or large squares could be cut from ⅜ yd. ¼ yd would be adequate for the little squares for either size. If you decide to make larger quilts, you will need proportionately more fabric.

Select a color scheme for the quilt. In each of our Railroad Crossing quilts, the fabric that made the small square established the dominant color and the one in the large square established the secondary color. Then 12 to 15 strip fabrics were selected to coordinate with both.

Reviewing the Variable Size Possibilities of the Grid System

Keep in mind that you determine the size of the pieces with any quilt design that can be drawn on a grid. Let's examine that thought more closely with the Railroad Crossing pattern.

Look at the photograph on page 23 or **Figs A, B**, and **C**. You surely already know we aren't going to cut those little pieces and sew them together. We will cut strips of random widths, sew the strips together along their long sides and cut the full set of strips into the length and width needed. Likewise, the squares are made from strips cut the same length as their width. But what size are they? What size do you want them to be?

Black and Tan Quilt

Navy, Lavender and Pink Quilt

While the black and tan quilt and the navy, lavender and pink quilt are different sizes, they are made with the same number of pieces. The pieces are proportionate. The two squares that determine the quilt's final size in the black and tan quilt are 5½" and 3" cut; and on the larger quilt they are 6½" and 3½" cut. Those two measurements determine the size of everything, except the borders. We intentionally made the borders proportionate also for a better comparison.

The point is that by only changing the cut measurement 1" and ½", the quilt is considerably larger. Approximate finished sizes are 31½" x 42" (black and tan) and 37½" x 50" (blue and pink). You could probably go to 7½" and 4" if you used lower contrast fabrics and the quilt would still not look too klunky and would be approximately 43½" x 57".

If you want the quilt to be bigger than that though, you would just add another row or two of blocks in the appropriate direction. See **Fig C**. The sizes mentioned thus far have all been measurements that would result in the large square being twice as big as the smaller one. That isn't necessary either, the squares could be a different proportion, like 6" and 2½", for example.

Another Lesson: Different Fabrics Equal Different Results

When making the quilts, the black and camel one was made first. Because these quilts were going to be used to visually show how making the pieces different sizes changed the final size, I was determined to make the quilts the same proportion, have parallel fabric arrangements, use the pieced binding on both, etc. Parallel fabric arrangements would mean that if the darkest fabric is positioned in the small square, the setting blocks and the second border on the first quilt, the darkest fabric would take the same 3 positions on the second quilt. I was trying to reduce the number of variables for the purpose of comparison.

Well, it's not that simple. When the second quilt top was finished, something made me uncomfortable. Finally, I cut some pink triangles and pinned them on top of the blue floral setting triangles. What a difference! Suddenly the diagonal pieced strips stood out instead of being lost in the floral print. Even though the top was complete and ready for quilting, we took the borders off and replaced the triangles. (For the first version, look at the small inset picture on page 23.)

When we got to the binding, the same thing happened. The striped binding which is great on the black and tan quilt simply didn't work!

The lesson is, don't be afraid to make changes as you go along. It is absolutely impossible to anticipate how everything is going to look together when you are working with so many fabrics.

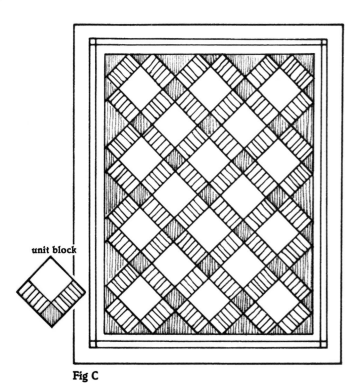

unit block

Fig C

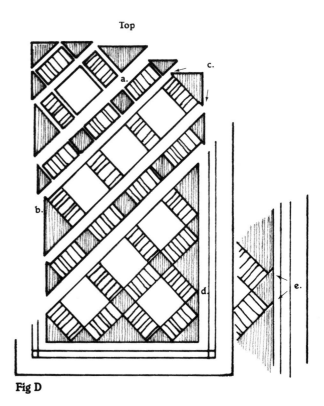

Top

Fig D

What is the Unit Block?

If you decide to make the larger quilt diagrammed in **Fig C** or one even larger, you will probably want to break the quilt into unit blocks. In **Fig C**, you can see there would be 15 complete unit blocks. If you are making the smaller crib or wall quilt, however, there would only be 6 complete unit blocks and 35 assorted sub-unit pieces. I think it is easier to abandon the unit block and to assemble the sub-units into the logical diagonal rows and then sew the rows together. Look at **Fig D** for layout and construction tips.

a. When the rows are going from the left side to the top of the quilt, the right angle corner lines up with the bottom of the square for seaming.

b. One triangle corner will extend above the rest of the row.

c. The corner triangles will have corners extending beyond the row width in two directions.

d. This placement shows "barely floating."

e. This shows "more floating."

Identify the sub-units and count the number needed. Your answer should look something like this.

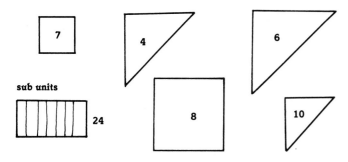

sub units

Read Secret of the Setting Triangles, page 30, before cutting triangles.

Cutting and Piecing the Setting Strips

Because the required amount of each print is so small, you may decide that it doesn't make sense to cut lengthwise strips. For any degree of efficiency in piecing, the strips should be at least 3 times as long as the chosen size of the small square. Quarter yard pieces of fabric cut on the lengthwise grain would qualify for the smaller quilt, but not the larger one photographed. For it, lengthwise strips of half yard pieces or "fat quarters" would be fine.

The width of the strips should be random. The smaller the square is going to be, the narrower the strips can be. Remember that once you take ¼" seam allowances on each side, a strip cut narrower than ⅞" will be barely usable. You also don't want a strip to end up so wide that it occupies the main part of the set.

With the Joseph's Coat border, we discussed the desire to camouflage the repeat of the strips. (You may want to review that section on page 25.) Several sets of shorter strips in different arrangements will accomplish this better than one arrangement of long strips. In this quilt, an easy trick is to make the set of strips slightly wider than the large square so that you can move the strip to the left or the right to have a different fabric seamed to the small square, **Fig E**.

Another way to help in this particular quilt is to mix the direction of the setting strips from each sewn combination. To accomplish this, cut one

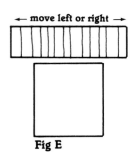

← move left or right →

Fig E

29

or two sections the width of the small square from each set of strips until you have eight. These are the sections that will be pieced with the strips perpendicular to the large squares. They will be sewn to the right side of the squares, so reverse some pieces, right sides down before stitching, **Fig F**.

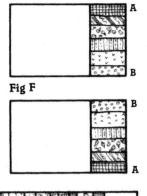

Fig F

You can save a piecing step if you cut a strip of the fabric for the small square instead of individual squares and stitch it to the remaining sets of strips. Then cut them together, **Fig G**.

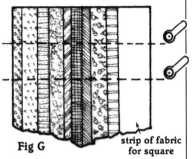

Fig G

strip of fabric for square

Add the Borders

I know there are a few things I repeat. One of them is that while border width measurements are included, they are not hard and fast "must use" measurements. They are just starting points. Borders and their relationship to each other and the quilt is what matters most and different fabrics relate to each other differently than those that might be pictured. For example, a very dark color generally looks heavier than a very soft pastel. It is almost assured that you will want to use them in different quantities. Fold fabrics into approximately border widths and lay them beside the quilt or even cut a few strips. Stand back and look, rearrange, try something else. Only if the quilt has to be an exact size to fit a certain bed or place could the actual size of the border be more important than the way it looks.

The cut width of the black/camel borders are 1¾", 1½" and 2¾". The cut width of the plum/pink quilt borders are 2", 1¾" and 3½".

The Striped Binding

Of special interest on the black and camel quilt is the binding. It was made just like the interior strips and was cut twice the desired finished width plus ½", in this case 2". It would have been too bulky to cut double as described in the last chapter. It was stay stitched ¼" from one edge. The other edge was placed right sides together on the quilt front and machine stitched in place ¼" from the quilt edge. Extra batting and backing had been allowed to extend beyond the quilt to be rolled into the binding as it was turned to the back and stitched in place by hand.

The Secret of the Setting Triangles

It's no secret that if you are trying to make a right angle triangle from strips or squares, you could get two triangles by cutting a square in half diagonally. However, when you are working in fabric and have grain lines to contend with, it could be difficult at best, disastrous at worst. Assuming the square was cut on grain, the hypotenuse of the new triangles would be a perfect bias and very stretchy.

To make setting triangles with the hypotenuse or long side on straight grain, we make a larger square and cut it in quarters diagonally, **Fig H**.

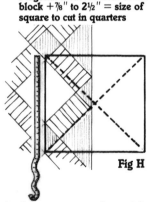

Diagonal measurement of unit block + ⅞" to 2½" = size of square to cut in quarters

Fig H

What size is the square you plan to quarter? Measure the diagonal of the unit block and add ⅞". That is the length of the side of the square you will quarter for a perfect, no mistakes fit, see **Fig H**. I prefer to make the setting blocks larger so that the design blocks float inside the borders instead of being crushed by them. For the starting square size for floating triangles, add 1½" to 2½" to the length of the diagonal of the unit block.

The 4 corner triangles can be cut from 2 squares the same size as the unit block, **Fig I**. They will be over sized enough to match large floating setting triangles. The excess can be trimmed away later.

Fig I

So analyze your right angle triangles. If you want the hypotenuse to be on straight grain, quarter a square diagonally. If you want the legs or short side to be on the straight grain, as in the corners of most diagonal set quilts, halve a square diagonally.

Sunshine and Shadows..........................

Rose Monochromatic Square Crib Quilt
approximately 51″ square

This is a fun, easy lap quilt or baby carrying quilt. It is also your introduction to unit block construction of the Sunshine and Shadows or Trip Around the World type quilt. With only six fabrics and the diagonal Sunshine and Shadows arrangement, it is quite easy to see and learn the principle of the unit block in what appears to be quilts with an all over design arrangement. A second construction method (more suitable for larger squares), the Cylinder Technique is shown in the Trip Around the World section on page 38.

FABRIC REQUIREMENTS

The quilt photographed is approximately 51″ square, including a 3″ and 4″ double ruffle. The strips for the square were cut 4″ wide, yielding 3½″ squares. Fat quarters (those 18″ x 22″ cuts available in lots of stores) would be perfect for the interior fabrics and the strips could be cut on the lengthwise grain. The quilt could easily be made with slightly smaller or larger squares and come out a considerably different size.

Backing fabric, 1¼ yd. It is fun to use the leftover fabrics from the front to make a simple pieced backing.

Ruffles
The 3″-wide muslin ruffle is a purchased, pre-gathered ruffle. 4⅞ yds are needed; I would buy 5 yds.

1½ yds fabric for larger ruffle. Doesn't that seem like a lot? Why would that be? To start with, it is a larger than average crib quilt. More specifically, however, the 4″ finished ruffle is a double ruffle gathered lightly, only about 1½″ to 1″ because it has the full ruffle on top. That means that since the quilt is almost 1¼ yds on each side, it requires 5 yds of gathered ruffle. At 1½″ to 1″ that is 7½ yds ungathered. If the ruffle is being cut on the crosswise grain, that is 7.5 times 36″ for 270 total inches of ruffle, divided by 45″ (the fabric width) to get 6. Six is the number of 9″ strips you will cut. Six strips x 9″ wide is 54″ divided by 36″ in a yard. You need 1½ yds of fabric for the wide ruffle.

FINDING AND MAKING THE UNIT BLOCK

Looking at **Fig A** you can see the breakdown of the 2 unit blocks A and B. They are modified Nine Patch units. Usually Nine Patch refers to two fabrics only, in an alternating checkerboard look. These Nine Patch units repeat the diagonal placement used in the whole quilt.

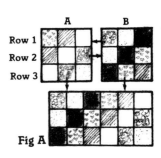

Fig A

31

Make the Nine Patch

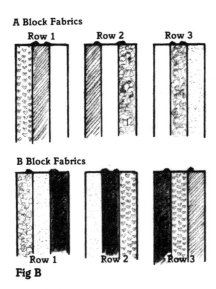

A Block Fabrics

Row 1   Row 2   Row 3

B Block Fabrics

Row 1   Row 2   Row 3
Fig B

Using the strip cutting and piecing techniques (**Fig B**), this is the set up for Unit Block A. Cut a strip instead of a square for each fabric in each row of the Nine Patch. Each strip should be as wide as the desired finished square plus ½". It should be long enough to cut either four or eight "second cut" strips. In this case, that measurement is the same as the width so it might be easier to say that these strips should be four or eight times as long as they are wide.

Seam the strips together in the proper order for each row of the Nine Patch. Press. On Unit Block A, press the seams on Rows 1 and 3 toward the center strips and on Row 2 toward the outside. For Unit Block B, do the opposite and then your automatic pinning, **Fig C**, will work throughout the whole quilt.

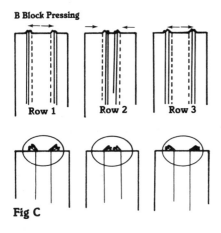

B Block Pressing

Row 1   Row 2   Row 3

Fig C

Directional pressing/automatic pinning is not always simple. It does however, make the patchwork so much easier and more accurate that thinking ahead is worthwhile. The more you piece, the more you will appreciate proper pressing.

After the rows are sewn and pressed, you are ready for the second cut—which actually completes the cutting of the individual squares—except they aren't individual anymore.

Thinking ahead again, an easy way to save a laborious step is to position the strips for Rows 1 and 2 right sides together. Because the fabrics are not arranged symmetrically, positioning them accurately is crucial. After placing the strips face to face, I always fold back the top layer to make sure the strips

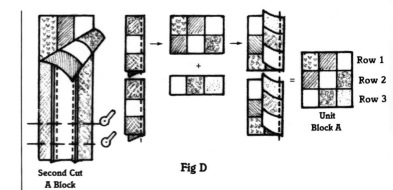

Second Cut
A Block

Fig D

Row 1
Row 2
Row 3

Unit
Block A

will be in the correct order when cut and sewn, **Fig D**. The ridges created by the directional pressing allow the strips to fit together snugly and without need for pinning, hence the name, automatic pinning.

Now cut both Row 1 and 2 together. Stack the pieces carefully. They are ready to go straight to the machine for seaming. Chain piece the sections and take an entire string to the ironing board. Press seam toward Row 1, clip threads and stack the new pieces in the identical order, one on top of the other. If you position the newly pieced and pressed sections so that Row 2 is on the right, it is already in the correct position for placing cut sections of Row 3 right side down on Row 2 and making the next seam, **Fig D**. When you are sure you've put the Row 3 section in the proper order, make all the rest of the units the same way, then they will all be right. It is smart to be doubly cautious on that first piece. If you make it wrong and then make all the others like the first one, you got it, they would all be wrong!

Assemble and Finish the Quilt

When you have completed the eight Unit Block A sets, make eight Unit Block B sets. Press seams down toward Rows 2 and 3 to continue automatic pinning.

Assemble the A and B blocks alternately as in **Fig E**. The decorative hearts randomly included were cut from printed fabric and fused in place after the quilt was pieced because I felt the quilt was borderline boring and needed a little something, **Fig F**. The fusing was done with one of the paper-backed fusible webs. When the quilt was machine quilted, the fused raw edges were zigzag stitched with the invisible thread to make the quilt very durable for washing.

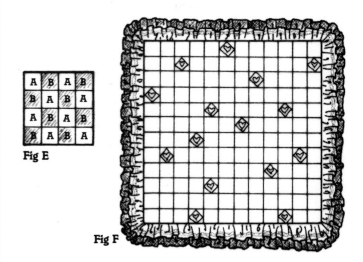

A	B	A	B
B	A	B	A
A	B	A	B
B	A	B	A

Fig E

Fig F

Cut the six 9" strips for the wide ruffle. Seam them together end to end. It is not necessary to seam the first and sixth strip into a circle. Press in half lengthwise. Gather. When quilting, do not quilt within the square next to the edge. (This quilt was machine quilted in concentric squares. No quilting lines crossed each other.) With backing hanging free from the quilt, pin both ruffles in place on quilt top. Stitch. Do not catch backing in the stitching. Extend ruffle away from the quilt so that seam allowances fold under the quilt top. Turn backing seam allowance under to cover raw edges and hand or machine stitch in place.

Basic Concept:
How to turn a Sunshine and Shadows into a Trip Around the World

If you divide a Trip Around the World quilt into four equal quarters, each section looks basically like a small Sunshine and Shadows quilt. The problem is that the diagonal direction of the blocks is different in two of the quarters and there is a center strip that could belong to either section. If you study **Figs G** and **H** carefully, you can see that if you made four sections just alike, rotated three of them and made center strips as diagrammed, you could quickly have a Trip Around the World quilt.

A Word of Caution: If the quilt is rectangular, two different sections are made, but they use all the same unit blocks. See illustration of Country Blue Trip Around the World on page 36.

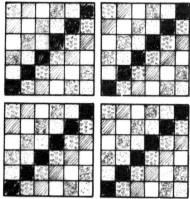

6 Fabric Sunshine and Shadow

Fig G

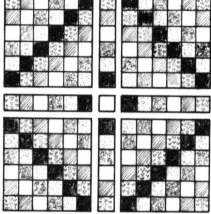

6 Fabric Trip Around the World

Fig H

Antique Sunshine and Shadow quilt, shown in color on page 21.

Antique Sunshine and Shadows

The Antique Sunshine and Shadows made with finished 2¼" squares is approximately 71" x 81", a little small by today's standards. The actual quilt is only 36 rows long. When you study **Fig I** you will see that we have made the quilt 40 rows long. This would make the quilt 71" x 90" with 2¼" finished squares; or with 2½" squares it would be 80" x 100", which is a perfect queen/double size.

Let's look at either the quilt or the diagram, **Fig I** on page 34. It is obvious that there is a repetitious pattern and that there must be a way to use strip techniques advantageously. This quilt has 2¼" finished squares (2¾" cut strips), nine different fabrics, repeated in a mirror image order twice. It can be made very easily using the Unit Block method. If you want to make a Sunshine and Shadows with larger finished squares you might want to use the Special Cylinder Technique shown in the Trip Around the World section, page 38.

Which is the Unit Block?

Because looking for repetition is stressed so much, it would be logical to assume that I would recommend making the biggest set of strips possible, but that is not necessarily so. **With the Antique Sunshine and Shadow quilt, we will examine several different ways to construct the same quilt. None of them are right or wrong. Different people like different methods.**

THE FULL REPEAT

The full repeat is 8 rows of 16 squares. That unit repeats 10 times in the quilt. If you were using that as the unit block you would make the appropriate set of 16 strips for each of the 8 rows. Each strip would be the chosen finished square size plus 2 seam allowances wide. The length of the strips would be 10 times the width. Then, when the strip sets were cut across, there would be one new strip for each of the 10 repeats. Each fabric, except fabrics 1 and 9, appears in every row twice so you would need to cut 16 strips of all fabrics except, 8 strips of fabrics 1 and 9.

You would sew the 16 strips for Row 1 together and press all the seam allowances to the right, then all 16 strips for Row 2 and press to the left, etc. Then you would make the "second cut" across the strips to make the appropriate rows of squares and sew them together. All of the seam allowances would be properly positioned for automatic pinning. As each section was completed, they would be sewn together so that the repeat would continue properly. When the 10 complete sets are done, they would be ready for final assembly.

Most combinations could be made with 8 rows of 16 squares, but eccentricities of this particular quilt require the two 8 by 8 sections shown in **Fig I** to keep alternating positions. The principle is the same, the rows just aren't as long. See **Fig J.**

PARTIAL REPEATS

If you look again at the full repeat, you will see it could easily be broken down to 8 by 8 square repeats or even 4 by 4. This would result in smaller, easier to handle units, even though it means multiple Unit Blocks as in the Rose Monochromatic quilt. If you choose either one of these repeats, they become the basis for your strip sets. When these smaller unit blocks are complete, you would assemble them into the 10 larger full repeats described above.

THE FOUR PATCH REPEAT

If the final squares were slightly larger and there were less of them, I would tend to use either of the subsets above, but for the quilt shown which has 1280 (don't panic!) squares, that are fairly small (2¼″ finished) I really love The Four Patch Repeat.

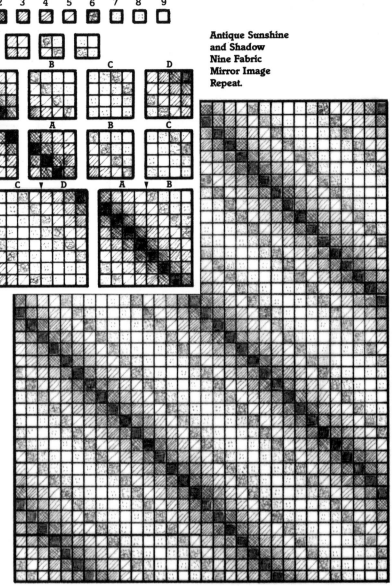

Antique Sunshine and Shadow Nine Fabric Mirror Image Repeat.

Four Patch Units

Partial Repeats

Full Repeats

Fig I

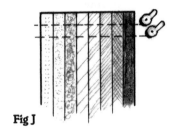

Fig J

34

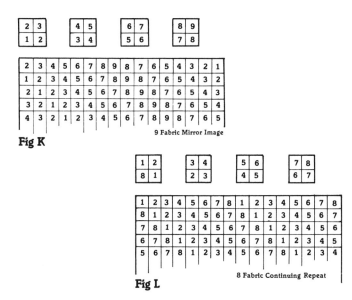

Fig K
9 Fabric Mirror Image

Fig L
8 Fabric Continuing Repeat

It's hard to believe that the entire antique quilt, using the mirror image repeat, is made of only 4 different Four Patch repeats. That has 9 fabrics in 16 positions, **Fig K**. If you select the 8 fabric continuing repeat, there are only 4 different Four Patches, **Fig L**. An easy way to check the repeat, is to give each position a number, and fill the numbers into a grid 8 squares high and 16 squares wide, **Figs K** and **L**. Now draw lines around Four Patch units to determine what your Four Patch units are.

The advantage of this method is that once you have determined your repeat and then established the 4 or 5 Four Patches that need to be made, it is very easy to sit and make the stacks of Four Patches. It takes very little space for any of the steps and is easy to control.

Making a Sunshine and Shadows Quilt

FABRIC REQUIREMENTS AND ARRANGEMENTS

Select eight or nine fabrics. The Master Diagram, **Fig I**, shows a 32 x 40 block grid. You need 9 fabrics to use the mirror image repeat shown on the antique quilt, **Fig K**. Eight fabrics repeated twice in the same order will also fit into this unit block repeat, **Fig L**.

To make the antique quilt with 2¼" finished squares, you will need ⅞ yd for each fabric that is used twice, less if it is only used once. Since I'm never positive of my arrangement and I don't like to feel like I might run out, I would buy a yard of everything.

In the antique quilt, the fabrics are mostly solids and the prints that are used are very tiny. This works fine with the smaller squares, but if you go to larger squares of solid color they look empty without lots of quilting. In that quilt, I particularly like the movement from light to dark, it gives an undulating look to the quilt. This particular quilt also is a good example of the illusion of "transparency" or looking through a color.

Look at all of the Sunshine and Shadows and Trip Around the World quilts. Try to ignore what actual colors the quilts are made in and study the fabrics of the quilts you like most to analyze contrast, blending, etc. Now translate that knowledge to choose the color family that you want to work with. As with most of the quilts, picking a favorite fabric that has several colors and using it to establish the color scheme for the rest of the fabrics is a helpful method for fabric selection.

MAKE A TRIAL LAYOUT

There seems to be no substitute for laying the fabric squares out to try the layout. No matter how many of these I make, I have yet to use the first layout plan. Eight rows by 16, or the full repeat, is enough to try. Your trial piece will be more visually accurate if you cut the squares the finished size, instead of including seam allowances. It does mean that the fabric can not be used in the quilt top, which is something to be considered if you are at all short of fabric. My preference is to cut finished size squares and then use a fabric glue stick to secure them in the selected layout to a piece of muslin.

Put your layout on a wall in your studio for ready reference. Remember, your studio is wherever you are creating. Calling that space a studio immediately elevates your image. So don't worry if you have to use the refrigerator and its full supply of magnets to hold this reference sheet in place. It is still your studio. Furthermore, if you don't have a space where you can leave this project in interim periods, you will really appreciate the reference sheet.

Make the Four Patches

Sew the first two fabrics together and press to the dark side. Repeat with appropriate fabrics for the second row and press seam so that it goes in the opposite direction. Position the two pairs of strips right sides together with adjacent fabrics touching, **Fig M**. Two 27" strips can be properly positioned almost as fast as two small pieces. Using the width of the individual strips as the increment, cut through both sets of strips, **Fig N**. They are cut in pairs, already properly prepared for the next seam. Stack them carefully and take the whole stack to the sewing machine and chain piece, **Fig O**. Take advantage of the automatic pinning developed from seam allowances pressed in opposite directions. It's so clever and it comes with The Four Patch Guarantee: "You can spend more time making Four Patches and you can do it with more difficulty, but you can't be any more accurate."

Following the diagram in **Fig I**, combine the Four Patch combinations into three different Sixteen Patch units. Put those together into the two 64 Patch units that make up the quilt. The only problem with the Four Patch Method is that directional pressing may be complicated.

See Finishing Your Quilt Top starting on page 40.

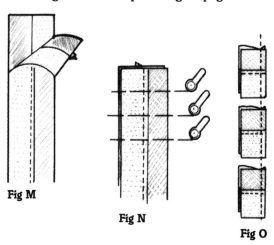

Fig M

Fig N

Fig O

...............Trip Around the World..............

While many people are fascinated with the lore of quilt names, I find them interesting, but am not compulsive about tracing the history of names, etc. However, it has fascinated me that this quilt is called "Step Around the Mountain" by some of my North Georgia long-time-quilter friends, and I've never seen it called anything but "Trip Around the World" elsewhere.

The Trip Around the World quilt starts out like the Sunshine and Shadows, but then the quadrants keep changing direction to make concentric diamonds in the quilt top design. This means that in most construction methods there is an extra row needed down the center, or one that is discarded from the repeat. But we still start with strips.

Let's look again at the diagram of the Sunshine and Shadows square crib quilt. See **Fig G** on page 33. First it is divided into quarters. Then three of the quarters are rotated, spread apart and center rows inserted in both directions, **Fig H** on page 33. The same principle applies here.

Country Blue Trip Around the World

queen/double, approximately 83½" x 100"

FABRIC REQUIREMENTS

It may be hard to believe, but the antique Sunshine and Shadow was the inspiration for this quilt. Yes, the color and style of the fabrics are very different, but the quilts are made with the same size square, the same number of fabrics and the mirror image repeat. This quilt was also enlarged with a 5½" border.

The fabric requirements for the Sunshine and Shadow and the interior of this quilt are the same, 1 yard each of 9 fabrics. You will need 2½ yds of border fabric if you want to have unpieced borders, and 1½ yds if you are willing to piece.

MAKING THE QUILT

As stated earlier, this quilt started out as a duplicate of the Antique Sunshine and Shadow quilt using 2¾" cut strips and the Four Patch block method. This combination requires 5 different Four Patch unit blocks, as illustrated in **Fig A**. When the Four Patch blocks had been combined into 16 square units, the quilt was laid out for viewing in both arrangements. It cried out to be converted to a Trip Around

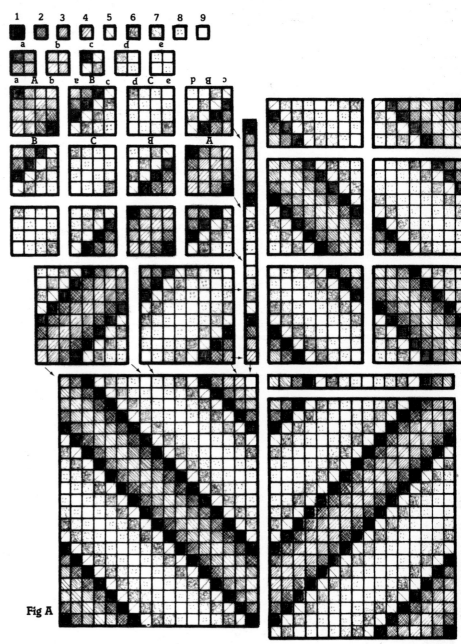

Fig A

the World. Because it was still in smaller units, they could easily be rearranged, accommodating the rectangular shape of the four sections in this quilt. The center strips were pieced from scraps and the quilt assembled. After the quilt was layered and quilted, the borders were added Quilt-As-You-Sew or Stitch and Flip method. The quilt features both free form quilting in the border and in the ditch quilting in the interior.

On one hand, you can develop a much more complicated surface design with smaller strips. The Country Blue quilt had 2¾" cut strips resulting in 1353 squares. On the other hand, you can get a great effect with larger strips in a lot less time. The Navy Richmond Hill quilt had 4¾" cut strips resulting in 357 squares. You decide which kind of quilt you want to make.

Country Blue Trip Around the World

81 X 96

Navy Richmond Hill Trip Around the World

Navy Richmond Hill Trip Around the World
queen/double approximately 86" x 102½"

FABRIC REQUIREMENTS

1 yd each of 9 fabrics for interior patchwork
2⅞ yds for a mitered corner border cut on lengthwise grain

Perhaps you have noticed, regardless of the size of square in the quilt the fabric requirement for each of the quilts with 9 fabrics has been 1 yd of each fabric. There is a safe rule of thumb for full-size Trip Around the World quilts with borders. Divide 9 by the number of fabrics being used. With 5 different fabrics in the repeat, you would buy 1¾ to 2 yds of each fabric. Don't forget to buy the border fabric, which is anywhere from 1½ yds to 3 yds depending on your cutting and construction techniques as previously discussed.

MAKING THE QUILT

Many people who started using strip construction methods for Sunshine and Shadows and Trip Around the World quilts would develop the fabric rotation and then sew all the sets of strips together in the same order with the same fabric first. When they had made the "second cut", the sets were all the same. So to get the desired rotation, squares would be taken off one end of the strip and sewn onto the other. It was easy to reverse pieces and make errors in the process. One solution is to make a different set of strips for every row (as described in the Sunshine and Shadows section with the full-size antique quilt). The Cylinder Method is another way to solve the problem. I especially like it for larger squares like this. It may seem strange, but it keeps the squares in order.

37

After the fabrics are picked and the rotation of colors decided, cut seven 4¾" strips of each fabric on the lengthwise grain, that is 36" long.

A time-saving cutting reminder: Before cutting, lay fabrics 1 & 2 right sides together, repeat with 3 & 4, 5 & 6 etc. The pairs of strips will be in the correct position for the first seam. Continue seaming sections together until the entire rotation of nine fabrics is complete.

Press half of the sets to the left, and half to the right. You will want to alternate these according to the row you are working on for automatic pinning. Using the same 4¾" width, make the "second cut" across the full set of nine strips until you have 42 sets (**Fig A**).

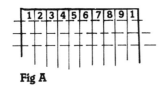

Fig A

CYLINDER METHOD FOR SUNSHINE AND SHADOW

Just as it was easier to understand the unit block method for a Sunshine and Shadow quilt and then transfer that understanding to a Trip Around the World layout, pretend for a moment that you want to make a Sunshine and Shadow quilt (**Fig B**). Using nine fabrics and this size square, two

Fig B

sets of strips could be sewn together at one end and the new strip, 18 squares long, would be wide enough for a Sunshine and Shadows quilt. Leave it flat, that is perfect for the first row. If you were to try to do that for the second row, the only way to get the diagonal arrangement of fabrics would be to take a square off one end of the strip and sew it to the other.

Instead, use the Cylinder Method. Sew the two sets of strips together at both ends to make a circle or cylinder. The cylinder is rotated until the correct fabric square is in line with the first square in row one, **Fig C**. Then it is time to remove the row of stitching that will allow the newly positioned fabric cylinder to become a flat row again. Put the new long rows right sides together, and with automatic pinning (directional pressing of seams) to hold the rows snugly in place, stitch. Rotate the next cylinder, remove the appropriate stitching and continue

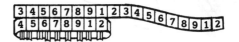

Fig C

in this manner for each row. Every ninth row has the correct fabric in the first position and does not need to be made into a cylinder.

CYLINDER METHOD FOR TRIP AROUND THE WORLD

How does the Cylinder Method apply to Trip Around the World? In this case, the quilt is really worked in halves. The cylinders are made from each cut set of nine squares. In other words there are twice as many cylinders. Of course, those rows that start with fabric 1 don't need to be sewn into cylinders. On one half of the quilt, a block is removed with every rotation to make the pattern work. See **Fig D**.

Layout of Navy Richmond Hill

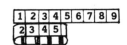

Fig D

FINISHING THE NAVY RICHMOND HILL

The very effective wide border (8½" cut—8" finished) means the finished interior squares can be large enough to make the quilt quickly, but small enough that it doesn't look like a beginner quilt. Because the batting selected for this quilt was an extra high loft, down substitute, comforter batt, it would have been impossible to have rolled it tightly enough to have quilted the entire thing at one time.

Instead the quilt was quilted in quadrants. The four sections were assembled and the raw edges finished on the back. Then the border, border backing and batting were seamed onto the quilt all at the same time as explained in Machine Quilting in Sections, page 43. You actually sew through all six layers at once, then pull the border sections away from the quilt and over the raw seam before adding quilting and binding to the borders. To go along with the comforter look, an unusually wide, ¾" finished binding was used.

38

Peach and Sea Foam Crib Quilt
approximately 38" x 50"

FABRIC REQUIREMENTS

¼ yd each of 6 prints
1½ yds for border—Border-printed stripe was cut on the lengthwise grain.

The strips were cut 3¼" wide. Odd measurements are easy when you are using the pattern free method and the rotary cutter system and tools. The quilt is 11 squares wide by 15 squares long. The larger the individual piece, the fewer needed to make the desired size quilt. Pieces cut too large can get klutzy, but an extra ¼" means a lot. The effective use of borders can also save a lot of piecing. No matter how good your methods are, if you can use fewer pieces effectively, it will take less time. The graceful printed border was conducive to having machine quilting follow along its design line, giving it a cable look.

Pink and Green Crib Quilt
approximately 32" x 41"

FABRIC REQUIREMENTS

¼ yd each of 5 fabrics
⅜ yd for border—These borders can be cut on the crosswise grain without piecing.

Let's compare this quilt with the previous one. It has the same number of pieces, but only a five fabric repeat. The starting strips are 2¾" wide, only ½" less than the previous quilt. The border is also proportionately smaller. But the quilt's finished dimensions are much smaller for basically the same amount of time, work and fabric—a perfect example of one of the repeated messages of pattern free quiltmaking. You decide what size. The large squares are better suited to the peach crib quilt than this color combination. The higher contrast ranging from the dark green to the light almost muslin color could make larger squares look klutzy.

Yellow Glendale Gardens Trip Around the World
queen/double approximately 79" x 100"

FABRIC REQUIREMENTS

The repeat in this quilt is actually a six fabric repeat, but the multi-colored floral was used twice to emphasize the color theme. The rule of thumb is too generous for this quilt because of the extra-wide border. Nine divided by six would be 1½ yds. In reality, with the 9½" border, only 1 yd of fabric is needed for each position—that would be 2 yds for the fabric that is used twice.

Because the border on this quilt was a border print and the corners are mitered, 10 running yards (the length around the outside edge of the quilt) of border print were needed. Fortunately, the border was printed on both sides of 60"-wide goods; so after purchasing 5 yds of fabric and cutting off the borders, there was still enough fabric left to make the quilt backing.

THE QUILT

The extra-wide decorative border was cut from a printed border fabric design. It has a dual purpose, it looks good and saves time. You could, of course, combine fabrics to get the multiple border effect, but the idea is to look for time-saving fabrics. This quilt has 391 squares. To get the same size quilt without a border would have required at least 240 more squares, not to mention that the border looks great hanging down the side of the bed.

This is another example of low contrast fabrics disguising the use of relatively large squares. The strips are cut 4" wide. Cut eight 4" x 36" long strips for each position. The quilt was made using the Cylinder Method for Trip Around the World.

39

Finishing Your Quilt Top......................

Now the Quilting

In Book One, we introduced straight line machine quilting "in the ditch" and a Quilt-As-You-Sew method for adding borders. This book will review those and add an introduction to free form machine quilting and machine quilting large quilts in sections.

The method I use most is machine quilting "in the ditch" and binding with a separate, straight grain, french fold binding (finished with blunt corners, not mitered). When tying, the only difference is a tied center section instead of quilted. Usually, I add borders "Quilt-As-You-Sew".

Preparation for Machine Quilting

WHY MACHINE QUILTING?

I love hand quilting, both doing it and looking at it. Hand quilting aficionados and anyone who has completely hand quilted anything, have a great appreciation for the hours of work. The uninitiated, however, almost invariably look at a hand quilted quilt, look at you and say "Did you do that by hand?" You beam, "Yes", then simply cannot believe the next question. "Couldn't they invent a machine to do that?"

They have. It's a sewing machine. You can't, of course, use any machine to make a hand stitch. The sewing machine stitch doesn't look like the hand stitch either. Until you get within a few feet or sometimes inches of a quilt, what you see is not the stitching, but the shadow created by the quilting indention. Machine quilting actually gives a crisper indention.

While I love hand quilting, I love making quilt tops more. I've learned, there's little personal satisfaction in a pile of unquilted tops. I also love having people use my quilts. I can do that with much more emotional ease when the quilts are machine quilted.

In the early years of the current quilt revival, machine quilting would hardly have been considered, but many people are more realistic today. It will change your life to begin thinking about appropriate times to machine quilt. Remember, everything's a trade-off. Piecing and quilting by hand, because it was once done that way and that is what you want to reproduce, is fine. Making quilts entirely by hand to make it a "real quilt" is not legitimate. Machine quilting is real. In fact, machine quilting may take more skill than hand quilting, but it is a different skill. It is also much faster.

It is true that while pioneer women quickly converted to piecing by machine, they were more reluctant to quilt by machine. I believe that they pieced by machine—something traditionally done alone—to have more quilt tops faster, yet quilted by hand in groups to preserve their social time. Quilting around the frame gave everyone a chance to hear the news, to gossip and to express themselves with other adult women. Lucky the quilter, today, who has a group to quilt with around a large frame. It is still fun and therapeutic. Lucky the quilter who can be comfortable with machine quilting, because that quilter will be more productive.

The quilts in this book are perfect for straight line machine quilting. Their straight design lines are easy to follow with machine stitching. In fact, these quilts practically beg to be machine quilted. While hand quilting can enhance any of the quilts, the overall graphic designs can stand alone without really missing the hand quilting. There are many opportunities for combining machine and hand quilting. Think about doing the long tedious seams and borders by machine, "in the ditch", and doing hand quilting in exposed blocks where it will really show!

Nearly everyone wonders if they need a fancy machine to do the quilting. I have successfully machine quilted with all kinds of machines from very simple to the most expensive. Check your machine's quilting I.Q. on scraps of fabric. If you have any problem, or don't like the look of the stitch, the first thing to check is the pressure of the presser foot. Too much pressure can make an undesirable rippling effect. Also, nearly every machine has an even feed attachment available that helps move all layers through the machine at the same rate. The second thing to check is thread tension. If you are using the invisible thread, it is almost always necessary to loosen the top thread tension.

Preparing the Backing Fabric

Because I prefer a separate binding, my backings need to be about two inches bigger in all directions than the quilt top and that is more for convenience than necessity. (If you want to bind the edges by bringing the backing around to the front, the backing size needs to be several inches larger.) On small crib or wall quilts it's usually not necessary to piece backings. The typical 45" wide fabric is wide enough and you just cut it slightly longer than the quilt. 60", 90" and even 108" wide fabrics are becoming more available to make unpieced backings for larger quilts. Some people try sheets for backings, but they are usually a tighter weave and most aren't 100% cotton. So, they could be considered an option for machine quilting, but they are definitely not recommended for hand quilting.

Usually a quilt back is made from one fabric with minimal piecing. Nothing says that has to be. In fact, I find more and more of my quilt backs incorporating some degree of patchwork, a trick that allows me to use up fabric from my reserves so I can buy new fabric for tops!

The most common pieced back is a single seam centered lengthwise, **Fig A**. Sometimes it is advantageous to make crosswise seams, **Fig B**.

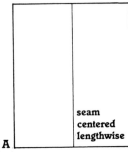

seam centered lengthwise

Fig A

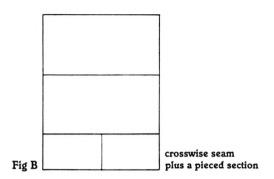

Fig B   crosswise seam
plus a pieced section

What Kind of Batting?

For machine quilting, my favorite batting is bonded polyester in a medium weight sometimes called all-purpose. As you are selecting batting, the important characteristics to look for are bonded throughout, not just surface bonding, and soft. Some bonded batts have given a bad name to bonded batting because they become very stiff. Machine quilting is also stiffer than hand quilting, so you want to start with as soft a batt as possible. Bonded throughout is important to help eliminate fiber migration. That's the term used to describe those little hairy fibers protruding through the quilt top, also known as bearding. A new black bonded polyester batting has just been introduced that will be very helpful in eliminating the bearding visibility on dark quilts.

There are typically three weights of batting available in the market place. They have different names, but generally speaking, there is the average weight batt used for most things. Low loft is used when you don't want much puff—usually used on garments and placemats, etc., and thick when you want extra loft.

Generally you want the all-purpose batting for machine quilting. Most people feel that the low loft does not add enough dimension to machine quilting. Thick batts are used when the end result you want is a comforter look. You might select that for tying, for example. If the batt is too thick, you may have to machine quilt in sections.

Machine Quilting "in the ditch"

Let's define "in the ditch," then we can quit putting it in quotes. "In the ditch" refers to stitching in the space created between two pieces of fabric that are sewn together. "What space?", you say. Granted there isn't much, so you create a little more space by applying slight tension. Your fingers won't just walk, they'll pull away from the seam as the sewing machine feed dog pulls the fabric through the machine. That slight tension creates the extra space for stitching. When your fingers release the tension, the fabric returns to it's natural position and tends to hide the stitching "in the ditch."

Materials Needed

At least one quilt top, batting and backing for layering. The backing should be pieced and pressed and the top pressed. Pay careful attention to the pressing and the direction of the seam allowances as you piece a quilt and this step will be easier. Measure to make sure the quilt's opposite sides are the same length.

A table. Not just any table. A relatively long narrow table is best. The necessary size of the table depends on the quilt size, but at least five feet long for a double or queen quilt. Wall hangings and crib quilts can be done on a smaller table. It does not work on the ping pong table. It does not work on the floor or a round table or a king size bed. It's nice if the table has a center crack, but if it doesn't, just measure and mark the center of both ends.

This table must not be a priceless antique, or even a pretty good one, because there is a great potential for scratching the surface of the table. You can put protective mats or a cardboard cutting board on a table, but it will be better if you can find a firm surface.

A friend. You can layer a wall hanging alone. You can do larger quilts alone, but a friend makes it easier and more fun.

Two yardsticks or tape measures.

Safety pins. The minimum number for a queen/double quilt is about 350 pins. A crib quilt will use at least 75, etc. I like rustproof chrome plated #1 pins—they're about ¾" long.

Invisible thread. Actually transparent is the word on most of the packages, but invisible sounds like more fun. It is a very fine nylon, not at all like the fishing line stuff available in the late 60's. It comes in clear and smoky. The smoky looks very dark on the spool, but one strand at a time, it's my favorite on everything but white and the lightest pastels. The clear reflects light on medium to dark fabrics.

You will develop a real appreciation for invisible thread when you are quilting a high contrast quilt. Let's say you are quilting "stitch in the ditch" style on a turkey red and muslin quilt, for example, and you have selected the red thread. Any place you miss and the red thread stitches on the muslin fabric, the stitches are visible from 30 feet in moonlight, and vice versa.

Regular sewing machine thread. Choose a color that matches the backing fabric and use it on the bobbin. I prefer cotton or a cotton wrapped polyester core. Matching or visible thread is okay on the top if the quilting is between low contrast fabrics or when all of the quilting is on only one color.

In the past, most threads called "Quilting Thread" were intended for hand quilting only. Now there are some very nice threads labeled for hand or machine quilting that I often use on the top when not using the invisible; but I still use the regular weight cotton thread on my bobbin.

The Actual Layering Process

After everything is gathered, the object is to center all three layers on themselves on the table. Center the backing fabric on the table wrong side up. Center it both lengthwise and crosswise. Using a lengthwise center seam or marked center line in the backing fabric as the guide, line it up with the center of the table. Compare until you and your friend have the same number of inches hanging off each end.

Add the layer of batting in the same way. Smooth it out carefully. Remove packaged batting from the bag a day or two in advance so it can relax. A careful steam press can eliminate difficult humps and bumps. Make sure the batting completely covers the backing fabric.

Fold the quilt top in half right sides together and lay the fold on the center line. Make sure the equal lengths drop off the ends. When that is accurate, carefully open the quilt top. (If you must work alone, mark the center of the table on the quilt batt, fold the quilt top in quarters and place the double fold at the center point, **Fig C**.) Open carefully.

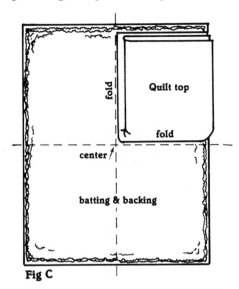

Fig C

Most quilt tops will be flat enough that you can just smooth them out. However, if you've had real problems piecing and the quilt top is very bumpy, you'll have to pat (in some cases pound) those bumps down. The fabric will scrunch up some in rough spots and you'll have to ease the top as you quilt, but it will look flat when you're through. If the bumps are really bad, you may have to shift to a fat batt! It truly will absorb the discrepancies better. The weight of the layers hanging off the table helps keep the fabrics smooth.

Start Pinning

How the quilt lays on the table, how it hangs and how you pin it will determine the position of all three layers when you quilt. Start in the middle and start pinning every four inches or in another selected pattern. Think about your quilting plan now so that you avoid pinning where you want to stitch. One of the real benefits of pinning rather than basting, is that you don't put your hand under the quilt and move it out of position. Just pin from the top. When you feel the pin point touch the table top, pull it back up through the quilt and close. Basting is more disruptive and takes longer. Straight pins are not an alternative because they catch on the quilt and scratch you badly as you are working. The number of pins per block or section depends on how many pins you have, how complicated the block is, etc. I recommend starting with more than you think you need and using less when you are more experienced.

Pin from the center out on the entire table surface. Pull the quilt to one side so that a new center section is on the table and work to one end. Every time you move the quilt, double check to make sure you haven't developed wrinkles or folds in the backing fabric. When that half is completed, go back to the center and start in the other direction.

Now what?

When you finish pinning, you are going to look at that quilt and say, "The part I still don't understand is how to get that great big quilt through the little opening in my sewing machine." That's right, the question is how do **you** stay in control instead of the quilt? The answer is to make the quilt smaller and more manageable.

The first seam to quilt is the longest center seam. Everything to the right of that seam as you sit at the sewing machine must go through the arch. Starting at the edge, roll that side up to within four or five inches of the seam. To the left of the seam, fold the quilt in several nine or ten inch folds until it is the same distance from the seam, **Fig D**.

Now it's a long thin quilt. Starting at the end opposite where you will start sewing, roll the quilt up like a sleeping bag, **Fig E**. Suddenly you have a manageable quilt. Carry it to the machine.

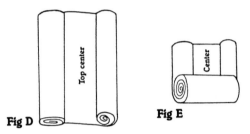

Fig D   **Fig E**

Setting Up the Machine

Invisible nylon thread goes on the top only. It is usually necessary to loosen the tension for the nylon thread. It is very stretchy and if the tension is too tight, the thread stretches while sewn and draws up and puckers when you finish.

While I like to use 10-12 stitches per inch for machine piecing, I change the stitch length to 8-10 stitches per inch for quilting.

Start Quilting

Sit at the machine with the rolled quilt in your lap. Position the quilt so that the end of the seam you are quilting is under the needle. Lower the presser foot and start quilting. With both hands, pull away from the seam to make the ditch. You'll discover forgotten muscles in your shoulders. Stop and relax your back and shoulders between rows. Keep the quilt loose enough that its weight doesn't pull against the needle. If your friend is there, you have a catcher. If not, you'll probably want a table in front of your sewing machine so the quilted section won't fall down and pull. When you have finished that seam, quilt the center horizontal seam. After that, I usually do two horizontal seams, one each side of center; then switch back to vertical, continuing to work out from center.

I hate to be the one to have to tell you, but you have to re-roll for every seam. Machine quilting goes in fast, but it isn't fast to take out. You want to stay in control of the quilt. As you re-roll, check the quilt back for newly sewn pleats. It's a personal decision, but I don't take out those little puckers most often found at seam crossings. If there's a tuck you could catch your toe in, you have to correct it. In between is a gray area.

Quilt-As-You-Sew Borders

Instead of adding borders to the quilt and then layering and quilting as described previously, only the patchwork interior of the quilt is centered on the full-size backing and batting. After that section is quilted, quilt-as-you-sew borders are added to the quilt. They are added just as they would have been except that you will sew through the batting and backing at the same time.

The point is, you have to make a seam to add the border to the quilt top center, so why not quilt at the same time? Measure and cut the quilt borders. Unless I have a fabric or design that demands mitering, I find crossed or blunt borders to be just fine. Add the side borders first and then the ends, just as if you were adding borders before layering and quilting. When there are several borders, I prefer to add them one fabric at a time to create more quilting.

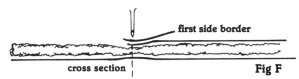

first side border

cross section   Fig F

After the quilt interior is quilted, put it right side up on a large flat surface. Put the first side border right side down on top of the quilt just as if you were making a regular seam, **Fig F**. Pin in place. Stitch through all thicknesses, quilting and seaming at the same time. Repeat with the opposite side border. Open new borders flat into the proper position before adding borders on the ends of the quilt. Pin or very lightly press the first border flat before seaming across the end of it with another border. Continue in the same order for each subsequent border.

Straight Machine Quilting that Isn't In The Ditch

Several of the quilts in this book incorporate regular or straight machine quilting on the surface of the fabric, rather than in the ditch. The only difference is that you have to mark a design or have a plan for the quilting and the stitching isn't hidden in a seam line. In the Peach and Sea Foam Crib Quilt, we followed the printed design in the fabric. In the Yellow Glendale Gardens Trip Around the World, the printed fabric was used as a guide for eyeballing the curving quilting line.

Free Form Quilting Adds Another Direction

Straight line quilting on the machine is really quite simple once you understand how to control the quilt and make it manageable. But what if you want to quilt in circles? Traditional sewing, where the feed dogs pull the fabric through the machine, would require somehow rotating that whole quilt around and through the machine. No way! So what happens if you disengage or lower the feed dogs? Well, basically, the needle goes up and down, but the machine doesn't move the fabric. That means you become the power moving the quilt under the needle and you can move it any direction you want, even in circles. The good part is you don't have to pivot the quilt around the needle!

That is why free form quilting is done with the feed dogs down. Most people like to replace the regular presser foot with the round embroidery or darning foot. When the presser foot is lowered, the darning foot doesn't actually touch the fabric, but it identifies where the needle will be stitching and is a safety buffer for your fingers. Even if you decide to stitch without a presser foot of any kind, the lever for the presser foot must be lowered as that is the same action that controls the tension on the upper thread.

Free form means what it says. You can stitch any direction you want. All of the quilts in this book that have free form quilting were done with random movements. If you were going to try fancy feather quilting on the machine, this method would be what you would use. Keeping the fabric moving at a fairly calm, steady pace and the needle moving fast seems to be the easiest way to keep your stitch length regular. The hardest thing to believe is that the faster you sew, the easier it is to do. Practice on a small piece of layered fabric, but remember, your stitch length will not have the same consistency as it does when the feed dogs and needle are completely synchronized.

The place you are most likely to get puckers in machine quilting is where two stitchings cross. A random motion that goes forward and curves back and cuts back again without actually crossing a previous stitching line will give you a nice quilted effect without puckers. Just a little practice and you'll be amazed at what you can do.

Use invisible thread or cotton thread that matches the major color in the fabric. There is less tension hassle with cotton thread. Remember to loosen your upper tension with the nylon thread. Your actual stitches are much less visible with the nylon thread.

Machine Quilting in Sections

While machine quilting techniques can be used on any size quilt, there is also a nice option for machine quilting a bed quilt in sections. In a nutshell, before completely sewing the patchwork interior together and adding the borders to the quilt, divide the number of squares into quadrants. They don't have to be equal in size, just have straight seams for combining later. At this point, your quilt will seem like four little crib quilts. Cut four backing pieces and four separate battings; layer and machine quilt as described, except stop a full ¼ " from the interior edges. It is okay to quilt to the edge where borders will be attached.

Put the quadrants together by putting right sides together and stitching through all layers; then trim away excess bulk and cover the seam with a bias strip. Or only stitch through five layers, leaving one layer of backing unattached. Trim away bulk and turn under backing and hand stitch in place to cover raw edges.

Now it is necessary to cut borders, border batting and border backing all as separate pieces. Lay the first side border face down on the quilt and pin in place. Turn this over and put the

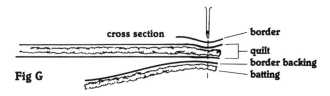

cross section   border
                      quilt
                      border backing
Fig G   batting

full width border backing piece right side down on the back. Put the batting on top of that. Pin these two layers in place. Stitch through all six layers. The entire quilt will be to the left of the needle, **Fig G**. Trim excess bulk from batting and seam, then pull all border layers away from the quilt and into their proper position. Repeat on the opposite side of the quilt and then do the ends.

If there are multiple borders, the additional borders would be added Quilt-As-You-Sew and the quilt would be ready for binding.

Because the Richmond Hill Trip Around the World had the very bulky, high loft batting, this was the method used for quilting it. Because the border backing pieces were cut separately, a contrasting fabric was used and a nice border created for the back of the quilt.

Making the Binding

The French fold binding is my favorite way to finish the edge of a quilt. It is cut four times as wide as the desired finished width PLUS ½" for two seam allowances AND ⅛" to ¼" more to go around the thickness of the quilt. The fatter the batt, the more you need to allow here. Fold the binding strip in half lengthwise with the wrong sides together and the raw edges even. Press.

Just like borders, I prefer to cut the binding on the lengthwise grain and I avoid piecing whenever possible. My favorite finished width is whatever size I think looks best with a large, high contrast binding. The most common, however, is about ½" finished. With that width and an average full-size quilt, the equivalent of ⅝ yd of fabric is required for bindings alone. If you don't want to piece the binding, the strips need to be cut from fabric as long as the quilt. There will, of course, be lots of fabric left.

In my opinion, bias binding is only necessary if the edge is curvy. Some people believe that bias will wear longer, but I don't have evidence to that effect. Even if it is accurate, does that justify the extra time it takes to make bias?

After preparing the binding, prepare the quilt. Usually I machine baste ¼" from the raw edge of the quilt top before trimming away excess quilt batting and backing.

Because I like full feeling bindings, I cut batting and backing that extends beyond the basting, almost, but not quite, twice as wide as the desired finished binding, **Fig H**. When the binding is stitched onto the quilt and pulled flat onto the batting, **Fig I**, it should be slightly wider than the batting.

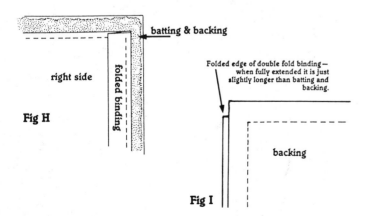

Lay binding on quilt so that both raw edges of binding match the raw edge of the quilt top and stitch in place. Roll binding around raw edge of quilt to the back, **Fig J**, and hand stitch in place using the row of machine stitching as a stabilizer and a guide. Add binding strips in the same order as borders.

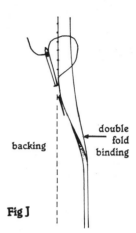

To make blunt corners (I feel mitered corners aren't necessary on most simple borders), add bindings on sides of quilt first and complete the hand stitching. Measure quilt ends carefully. Add ½" at each binding end. To eliminate raw edges, turn that ½" back on the wrong side before stitching in place.

The hand hemming stitch I use is hidden. The needle comes out of the quilt and takes a bite of the binding and reenters the quilt exactly behind the stitch. The thread is carried in the layers of the quilt, not on the outside. At the corners, trim away enough batting and seam allowances to make the corners feel and look like the same thickness as the rest of the binding. Carefully stitch ends shut.

MACHINE HEMMED BINDING

If you are hemming the binding by machine, attach binding to back and bring to front and either top stitch with invisible thread or experiment with your machine hemming stitch.

NO SEPARATE BINDING

The gray Amish Shadows quilt was finished by turning the quilt's border from the front to the back of the quilt. At least an inch of extra border must be allowed if it is your intention to finish a quilt this way. Carefully hand stitch, avoiding catching any of the fabric on the front of the quilt.

When finishing by bringing extra backing fabric to the front, the backing fabric must be selected to compliment the quilt. If I finish a quilt this way, I make sure that I stitch through the backing fabric to make the edge sturdier.